Divine Redemption
and the
Refuge of Faith

By the same author:

Christian Confession and the Crackling Thorn: The Imperatives of Faith in an Age of Unbelief
The Fracture of Faith: Recovering Belief of the Gospel in a Postmodern World
The Bondage of Grace
Man in the Maelstrom of Modern Thought: An Essay in Theological Perspective
Now That You Have Believed: An Exploration of the Life and Walk of Faith
Christian Truth in Critical Times
Studies in the Theory of Money 1690-1776
A Study of Mutual Funds (with Irwin Friend, F. E. Brown, and Edward S. Herman)
The Theory of the Firm: Production, Capital, and Finance
Financial Markets in the Capitalist Process
Economics and Man
A Christian Approach to Economics and the Cultural Condition
Money Capital in the Theory of the Firm
Money, Banking, and the Macroeconomy
Economics and the Antagonism of Time: Time, Uncertainty, and Choice in Economic Theory
The Tyranny of the Market: A Critique of Theoretical Foundations
Economics and Ethics: An Introduction to Theory, Institutions, and Policy

Divine Redemption and the Refuge of Faith

The Gospel of Grace Confronts the Human Condition

Douglas Vickers

REFORMATION HERITAGE BOOKS
Grand Rapids, Michigan

Copyright © 2005
Reformation Heritage Books
2965 Leonard St., NE
Grand Rapids, MI 49525
616-977-0599 / Fax 616-285-3246
e-mail: orders@heritagebooks.org
website: www.heritagebooks.org
ISBN 1-892777-40-1

All rights reserved. Printed in the United States of America.

For additional Reformed literature, both new and used, request a free book list from the above address.

Foreword

The time-honored theology that the Reformation bequeathed to us is now being discounted even in many evangelical churches. New perspectives challenge old verities. The need to return to biblical foundations is urgent. In *Divine Redemption and the Refuge of Faith*, Douglas Vickers has raised the pressing questions: Who is Jesus Christ? What is the human condition? And in what respect is that human condition addressed by the presence of Jesus Christ in the world?

In lucid and arresting terms, Dr. Vickers provides answers developed from three basic theses that structured Reformation thought:

• the claim of Athanasius against the Arians and the Sabellians that the self-existing, autotheotic Second Person of the Godhead came as Jesus Christ;

• the doctrine of Augustine who rightly argued against Pelagius that the human will was bound in sin as a result of Adam's fall; and

• the teaching of Anselm who returned theology to its biblical roots when he claimed that Christ in his atonement provided a necessary and complete satisfaction for sin.

Divine Redemption and the Refuge of Faith provides a biblical-theological corrective to contemporary doctrinal deviations. It is recommended to all who are committed to the unchanging truths of the Christian confession, and will be of substantial benefit to Christians seeking a biblical explanation of the state of affairs in the world and in the church, as well as to theological students and the academic community.

Vickers is a native of Australia and graduate of the University of Queensland, who went on to complete a Ph.D. in economics at the University of London in 1956. He embarked on a teaching career, teaching finance at the University of Pennsylvania (1957-1972), and economics at the University of Western Australia (1972-1977) and the University of Massachusetts (1978-1995). At present he is professor emeritus of economics, University of Massachusetts.

Along the way, Vickers found time to pursue a long-standing interest in Reformed theology, first as a member of Westminster Presbyterian Church in Australia, and today as a member of First Congregational Church of Millers Falls, Massachusetts. He has been an active participant in the proceedings of the Reformed Congregational Fellowship and the New England Reformed Fellowship. The author of numerous books and papers on economics, Vickers has used his considerable skills in the research and writing of Reformed theology and Christian apologetics, this work being the latest from his pen. His most recent work, *Christian Confession and the Crackling Thorn: The Imperatives of Faith in an Age of Unbelief* (also published by Reformation Heritage Books), has been appreciated by many.

Vickers knows his subject – not only from ongoing study and careful reflection, but also by genuine personal experience of the truth of the gospel of our Lord Jesus Christ as "the power of God unto salvation, to every one that believeth" (Rom. 1:16). Once again, he has given us a book that presents Reformed convictions in large, biblical terms that get to the heart of vital Christianity. His approach is rooted in the writings of Cornelius Van Til, formerly professor of apologetics at Westminster Theological Seminary, who has had a profound impact on Vickers's thinking over the last several decades. If you are looking for a clear-headed, sure-footed, and warm-hearted guide on the cardinal issues of Christianity in every age, read this book repeatedly. It will provide you with solid theological moorings in a world that is groping in the dark for truth.

--Joel R. Beeke
Puritan Reformed Theological Seminary

Author's Preface

The observation that we live in a secularized, post-Christian age is rescued from the commonplace by the seriousness of its import. The twentieth century that limped to its conclusion has bequeathed the problem that modern man has lost a clear view of his status and his place. The logic and gathering momentum of modern thought has fathered a new humanism and has set the stage for a complete devolution of thought away from earlier and secure moorings. A new paganism casts its deadening shadow in the land. But in the tortured conundrum of the human condition man will not, because he cannot, see that his problem is insoluble outside of the terms of the Christian revelation.

My objective in this book is to raise a number of questions that press with some urgency on the contemporary theological and cultural state of affairs. The human condition is what it is by reason that we have inherited the effects of our first parents' repudiation of their covenantal obligations. Those obligations devolved upon them by virtue of their creation in the image of God. I have therefore looked with some care at the terms of the pristine covenant of works and the promises it contained of blessing and benediction in response to obedience, and of curse and malediction in the event of disobedience. But the covenant of works has fallen on hard times in the theological literature, and I have addressed the principal grounds on which a dissent from the doctrine has been made. It is necessary to see that the explanation of the coming of the Son of God into the world is that he came as the sinner's substitute to fulfill the previously unfulfilled obligations of the covenant of works. In that, he was our substitute prophet, priest, and king.

The good news of the gospel is that God has set forth for his people a redemption from sin. Against the disabilities of soul that characterize man in his fallen condition, the darkness of the mind, the distorted hatred of the heart, and the bondage of the will, redemption was accomplished by none other than the incarnate Son of God, and it radiates its meaning to the cosmic significance of Christ. In his substitutionary obedience and sacrifice we have what I have referred to as the "Refuge of Faith." By faith alone, which is the gift of God, the believer is assumed into union with Christ and thereby into the community of the church of which Christ is the Head. For this reason I have spoken of the identity and office of the church. The primary office of the church is the evangelistic preaching of the gospel and the nurture of the saints. As to possible involvement in cultural and economic affairs, I have differentiated between the office, prerogative, and responsibility of the church as the church on the one hand, and that of Christian people as individuals on the other.

The doctrines I have discussed have recently come under attack in the theological literature. I have therefore noted briefly the neo-Socinian claims of Open Theism, or the openness of God, and in a lengthy footnote at the end of the final chapter I have drawn attention to some of the principal propositions and concerns of what has become known as the New Perspective on Paul.

My thanks are due for the assistance I have received from a number of people in writing the book – to Dr. Joel. R. Beeke for his editorial comments and his generous foreword; Rev. Ray Lanning for his reading of an initial draft; Rev. Dr. Robert E. Davis for his encouragement and help that extended beyond the normal demands of his pastoral responsibilities; Ann Hopkins for her editorial assistance, a ready help that has now extended over many books and academic projects; and my wife, Miriam, for her support under the pressures that the life of an author imposes. I absolve all of these people from responsibility for the infelicities that may remain in the work.

Contents

Foreword by Joel R. Beeke	v
Author's Preface	vii
1. The Contemporary Condition	1
2. The Prelapsarian Covenant	26
3. The Dissent from the Covenant of Works	48
4. The Status of the Will and the States of Human Consciousness	74
5. The Possibility of Redemption	106
6. The Cosmic Significance of Christ	128
7. The Church: Its Identity and Office	149
8. The Issues Revisited	175
Index of Scripture References	187
Index of Names	191
Index of Subjects	195

Chapter 1

The Contemporary Condition

The twentieth century, heralded in the high glow of optimism as the century of the common man, has left its noblest hopes unrealized. It limped to its conclusion and bequeathed an age that edges to cultural collapse. Its unsolved problem, that modern man has lost a clear view of his status and his place, continues to haunt the best endeavors at explanation. It is insoluble outside of the terms of the Christian revelation. Man in the large, engulfed in the clichés of a scientific humanism, has surrendered man the individual to a cipher, a digit in the ironic dehumanized outcome that science, too large for morality, conceived. The materialism we have worshiped has trapped us in its spiritual emptiness.

The hypotheses of progress and perfectibility are sobered now. Brave imaginations of evolutionary thought had earlier joined the contemplations of biological and socio-cultural betterment. But now the century that announces the third millennium since the watershed of all of human history remains innocent of solutions, or even, it might be judged, of a sound diagnosis of its condition. The questions remain. Why is the state and condition of man what it is? Is there no escape from the torture of wars abroad and crime at home, and from the agonies of poverty, of economic slump, inequities, and exploitation? Is there no resolution of the humiliations born of the clash of ideologies and of movements of man in the mass that submerge the sensibilities adequate to express the true dignity of man? Is it any longer adequate to say that man has come from the mud? What, now, is to be said of the erstwhile hopes for the infinite perfectibility of man? The diagnostic bankruptcy of the contemporary non-Christian humanism presses its claim on sobered opinion.

The inner logic and the gathering momentum of modern thought have fathered a new humanism, the grandchild of the philosophic enlightenment of the eighteenth century and the positivist and scientific methodology it fostered. That hapless descendant, embarrassed by the fading of the crass aspirations of human betterment it conjured, has set the stage for a complete devolution of thought away from its earlier and secure moorings. There is now no fear of God in our cultural contemplations. In our secularized post-Christian age a new paganism casts its deadening shadow in the land. Forsaken by his fading dreams, his thirst unslaked by the broken cisterns he patronized, man is alone now, without hope, in a blind alley and dead end of despair. But in the tortured conundrum of the human condition he will not, because he cannot, see that his answer lies in an appeal to the God of all grace from whose hands he came. He does not, because he will not, see that he is the creature of a Creator-God to whom he sustains unalterable obligations and to whom he is ultimately accountable, for eternal good or woe. Is the best that man can say, "I have nothing to look forward to but chill autumn and still chillier winter and yet I must somehow try not to lose heart"?[1]

---

[1] Attributed to Dr. Marrett of Oxford, quoted in Selwyn Hughes, "I'm afraid of the dark" (in www.galingpilipino.com/ html/devotions.html).

Or do we have nothing to guide us beyond the pessimistic *Mind at the End of its Tether*, the final book that H. G. Wells published in 1945, the year before his death in his eightieth year? Have we made no progress beyond that earlier declaration of despair?

The church, when it is true to its calling, announces that the answer to the distress and the hopelessness of the human condition lies in the biblical revelation of God's redemptive purpose. The threefold rubric of creation, fall, and redemption radiates to an explanation of the sovereignty and authority, the transcendence and immanence, and the gracious purposes of the creator-God; it addresses the enslavement to sin in which humanity was captured by Adam's fall; and it discloses the prospects of rescue and redemption provided by the entrance into time of the eternal Son of God. The theological mind, when it is properly alert to its task, moves in an orbit structured by its captivity to the Word of God. That orbit is formed at its apogee by the reality of the glory of the triune God, and at its nadir lies the reality of the human condition as we are now addressing it. Reflective minds wrestle with the questions that engage those contrasting conceptions. The corresponding enquiry is capsulated in the cry of Job "How should man be just with God?" (Job 9:1). No more important question engages human enquiry, and no more urgent question presses on theological reflection.

The explanation of the human condition and the prospects for its rescue lie in what is involved in the messianic-redemptive accomplishment of Christ. At this initial stage, and before we consider in more detail what is apposite in God's inscripturated revelation, let us look briefly at three issues of doctrinal relevance. They have to do with, first, the being of the Person of Christ who came into the world to redeem his people from the entailment of their sin; second, the state of man as he exists by reason of the imputation to him of the guilt of Adam's sin, as that follows from the fact that Adam was established as the federal head and representative of the race; and third, the essential meaning of the rescue from sin that Christ accomplished in the atonement he provided in accordance with the Father's will and purpose. In that manner, our immediate concern with the contemporary human condition will be seen to be sandwiched between the being of the Savior of men on the one hand and the method of his salvific accomplishment on the other.

Athanasius, Augustine, and Anselm, to put them and their principal contributions in chronological order, stand as early scholars who addressed our threefold questions. They flourished before the revival of biblical theology that marked the Protestant Reformation of the sixteenth century. On October 31, 1517, Martin Luther nailed his 95 Latin theses to the door of the church at Wittenburg, and those theses "were copied, translated, printed, and spread as on eagles' wings throughout Germany and Europe in a few weeks."[2] That date has ever since been celebrated as Reformation Day. The church stands on the Scriptural integrity of Luther's claim that we are justified by faith alone (Rom. 1:17). The faith that is "the gift of God" (Eph. 2:8) is the *instrumental* cause of our salvation, while the grace of God is the *efficient* cause, and the obedience and sacrifice of Christ is the *meritorious* cause. The Reformation accomplishment clarified the biblical declaration that the sinner's salvation is by grace alone, through faith alone, in Christ alone. In the perfect substitutionary work of Christ for sinners is the refuge of faith.

John Calvin is properly regarded as the foremost theologian and exegete of the Reformation, and his *Institutes of the Christian Religion*, first published in an initial form in 1536, appeared in its final and expanded edition in 1559.[3] The theology of the Reformation received a highly important

---

[2] Philip Schaff, *History of the Christian Church* (Grand Rapids: Eerdmans, 1979), VII:156.

[3] John Calvin, *Institutes of the Christian Religion*, trans. F. L. Battles, ed. J. T. McNeill (Philadelphia: Westminster Press, 2 vols., 1960).

English language formulation in the seventeenth century at the hands of such scholars as John Owen and Thomas Goodwin, and a large number of Puritan preachers, including John Flavel, Thomas Manton, William Gurnall and others too numerous to mention.[4] It came to confessional statement in the Westminster Confession of Faith in the 1640s, the Savoy Declaration of Faith in 1658, and the Baptist Confession in 1689, and is celebrated in the commentaries of Matthew Henry[5] and Matthew Poole.[6] In the same century the flowering of Reformed theology was given prominent expression in Holland by Herman Witsius,[7] and in Geneva by Francis Turretin.[8]

But the expansive literature of Reformed theology stands on the shoulders of Athanasius, Augustine, and Anselm. They are referred to at this point, not in order to give a full treatment of their work or their historic importance, but to bring to emphasis the threefold issues bearing on our present discussion. Athanasius stood for the defense of the doctrine of the autotheotic nature of Christ as the Second Person of the Godhead. Augustine defended the biblical revelation of the state of man in sin and the incapacities of soul that attended his fallen condition. And Anselm gave us an early statement of the necessity for the atonement and of the "satisfaction theory" of the atonement of Christ, or the fact that in his atonement Christ satisfied the justice of God by bearing the penalty for the sins of his people.

---

[4] Works by the authors mentioned have been republished by the Banner of Truth, Edinburgh.

[5] Matthew Henry, *An Exposition of the Old and New Testaments*, various editions.

[6] Matthew Poole, *A Commentary on the Holy Bible* (London: Banner of Truth, 3 vols., 1962).

[7] Herman Witsius, *The Economy of the Covenants between God and Man* (Phillipsburg: Presbyterian and Reformed, for the den Dulk Christian Foundation, 2 vols., 1990).

[8] Francis Turretin, *Institutes of Elenctic Theology* (Phillipsburg: P&R, 3 vols., 1992-1997).

Athanasius and the Arian and Sabellian controversies

In the early history of the church the two quite different heresies of Arianism on the one hand and Sabellianism on the other attacked the doctrine of the consubstantiality within the Godhead of the Father and the Son. It is readily understandable why the doctrine of the Person of Christ should have been the early point of attack. For if what was believed of the Person of Christ were to be destroyed, and if the biblical data on that point were to be successfully refuted, then the whole of the newly established Christian religion and the prospects for the Christian church would be at once eliminated.

The followers of Sabellius, a presbyter of Ptolemais in the years 250-260, admitted that a distinction in the Godhead is set forth in Scripture, but the Sabellian system of thought denied that the distinction was a personal one. It asserted, in other words, "that the Father, the Son, and the Holy Spirit are just three different names for one and the same person, viewed under different aspects or relations."[9] The distinction within the Godhead, the Sabellians claimed, was "merely nominal or modal."[10] Put differently, Sabellius understood by "the Logos [the Son] and the Holy Spirit two Powers (δυνάμεις) streaming forth from the divine Essence, through which God works and reveals himself."[11] While Sabellianism did not become an accepted part of the dogma of the church and was held only by certain individuals, Athanasius rejected that erroneous doctrine. Shedd sums up his critique by saying that "He describes the Sabellian trinitarian process as a 'dilatation and contraction,' an 'expanding and collapsing' of the Divine Essence."[12]

---

[9] William Cunningham, *Historical Theology* (London: Banner of Truth, 1960), 1:272.
[10] Idem.
[11] W. G. T. Shedd, *A History of Christian Doctrine* (New York: Charles Scribner's Sons, 2 vols. 1868), 1:257.
[12] See ibid., 260-61.

Athanasius stood strenuously also against the virulent heresy that had been promulgated by Arius, a presbyter of Alexandria in the early fourth century, and that had been condemned by the Synod of Alexandria in 321. It was addressed and again condemned at the Council of Nicea in the year 325. At issue again was the doctrine of the consubstantiality of the Son with the Father. The Nicene Creed asserted that "the Son was 'homoousios' [of the same substance] with the Father ... [and] ... that He was begotten of the substance of the Father, and, of course, had a substance not only the same in kind, but numerically one with His."[13] The "homoousios" doctrine had been earlier deduced and stated by Alexander, bishop of Alexandria, in opposition to Arius. Against the Arian heresy, the doctrine was thereby stated that while there exists three Persons within the Godhead and each Person is characterized by distinguishable properties, it is to be said and maintained that the divine nature, the divine essence, exists fully in each of the Persons.[14] God the Son possesses fully the one divine nature. He is himself fully God. In that manner Nicea insisted on the autotheotic nature of the Son of God.[15]

The Arians dissented from that well-formulated doctrine.

---

[13] Cunningham, *Historical Theology*, 1: 284.

[14] We say that the "distinguishable property" of the Father is that he generated the Son from all eternity, and that the "distinguishable property" of the Son is that he was begotten of the Father. It is the "distinguishable property" of the Holy Spirit that he proceeded from the Father *and* the Son. That last-mentioned point of doctrine, as to the procession of the Holy Spirit, became a matter of dispute between the Eastern and the Western churches, denied by the former and maintained by the latter, and was incorporated definitively in doctrinal formulation by the Council of Toledo in the year 589. It has been referred to subsequently as the *filioque* clause.

[15] Turretin discusses the relevant doctrines and observes that "Although there are more persons than one in God, yet there are not more natures. All Persons partake of one and the same infinite nature, not by division, but by communication" (*Elenctic Theology*, 1:182).

For them, the Son was not "homoousios," but "homoiousios." Note that the insertion of the "i" (the Greek iota, ι) changes the meaning of the statement from "of the same substance with the Father" to that of being "like the Father." The import of the Arian claim was that the Son did not participate in the primary essence of the Father. The Son, Arius claimed, was "not divine in any sense, but is strictly a creature, though the very highest and first of all."[16]

Leaving aside for the present a fuller inspection of these early Christological controversies, it was established by the church at the Council of Nicea that it was necessary to maintain the consubstantiality of the Persons of the Godhead. That conclusion followed from the clear testimony of the Scriptures. The essence of God existed fully in each of the Persons. The Son, who executed his messianic-redemptive mission in this world in his human nature, is fully God. It is on that point that Athanasius insisted strongly, and it is to him that we are indebted for the principal defense of the doctrine in the years that followed.

The immediate relevance of what has been said is that the atonement that Christ offered for the sins of his people was, in fact, offered by the very Son of God. In that there shines the ultimate demonstration of the love of God for the people he chose to redeem (Eph. 1:4); they are "the church of God, which he purchased with his own blood" (Acts 20:28). The meaning of redemption is that God the Father set his love upon us and "sent his Son [from his eternal bosom and from the glory which the Son had with him "before the world was" (John 17:5)] to be the propitiation for our sins" (1 John 4:10).

---

[16] Shedd, *History*, 1:307. See Shedd's extended discussion of the early Christological controversies. At op. cit. 258 Shedd provides a significant comment on the respects in which the Sabellian view of Christ differed from that of the Arians. The former did not, as did the Arians, claim that Christ was an ordinary man. For them, "the Logos-Power entered into *union* with Christ's humanity, and not merely inspired it." Shedd, loc. cit.

In sending his Son into the world God set his love upon those who were the objects of his wrath.

The question of the autotheotic nature of Christ, the eternal Son of God, was confirmed and settled in creedal form by the Council of Chalcedon in the year 451. It was concluded there that in his coming into the world God the Son took into union with his divine nature a fully human nature. As the Westminster Shorter Catechism puts it, "The only redeemer of God's elect is the Lord Jesus Christ, who, being the eternal Son of God, became man, and so was, and continueth to be, God and man, in two distinct natures, and one person, forever." And "Christ, the Son of God, became man, by taking to himself a true body and a reasonable soul, being conceived by the power of the Holy Ghost, in the womb of the Virgin Mary, and born of her, yet without sin."[17] The apostle to the Romans holds clearly to the deity of the Son in his statement that "Christ ... is over all, God blessed for ever" (Rom. 9:5). And "In him dwelleth all the fullness of the Godhead bodily" (Col. 2:9). In his bodily, human nature the Son of God suffered for his people in his active obedience, and in his passive obedience he died his substitutionary death on the cross. In that human nature he rose triumphant over death and the grave and ascended to the right hand of the Father. Now in his full divine and human personhood he discharges his heavenly High Priestly office and function.

The Christological settlement of Chalcedon is summarized by saying that the divine and human natures were joined in union in Christ, without confusion, without change, without division, and without separation. The first two of those descriptive terms insist on the fact that there was no intercommunication of properties between the divine and the human natures. At the incarnation, when Christ took to himself the created human nature that had been prepared for him, there was no commingling of the eternal and the tempo-

---

[17] Westminster Shorter Catechism, Questions 21, 22.

ral. The second two of the terms describing the Person of Christ insist on and guard the reality of the union.[18]

Augustine and the Pelagian controversy

Our brief comments on the significance of Augustine will exhibit the basic and essential explanation of the contemporary human condition. That is because the points at issue in the controversy between Pelagius and Augustine were addressed to the question of the ability status of man as he exists after, and as a result of, Adam's fall. We are interested now in man's postlapsarian condition. What, in other words, is to be said on the basis of the Scriptural data of the effects on, and the implications for, the faculties of the soul as a result of the Fall? First, the guilt of Adam's first sin was imputed to all those who descended naturally from him. "The covenant [the covenant of creation, also referred to as the covenant of works] being made with Adam, not only for himself, but for his posterity, all mankind, descending from him by ordinary generation, sinned in him, and fell with him in his first transgression."[19] The "by ordinary generation" clause protects the sinlessness of Christ in his human nature and his impeccability in his person. Secondly, a sinful human nature was transmitted from Adam to his descendants, again to those who descended from him by ordinary generation. The twofold implications of Adam's fall, the imputation of the guilt of his sin and the transmission of his fallen nature, take up the entailment of that first sin. "I was shapen in iniquity," the Psalmist says, "and in sin did my mother conceive me" (Ps. 51:5). And our Lord made it clear to the dissembling Jews on one occasion that "Ye are of your father the devil, and the lusts of your father ye will do" (John 8:44).

---

[18] See Cornelius Van Til, *The Defense of the Faith* (Philadelphia: Presbyterian and Reformed, 1963), 16-17.
[19] Westminster Shorter Catechism, Question 16.

We have referred in the foregoing to the early *Christological* controversies, those related to Sabellianism and Arianism. Now in the debate between Pelagius and Augustine an *anthropological* controversy comes to the fore. The first issue dealt with the person and nature of Christ. The second addresses the nature and the capacities of soul of man.

Pelagius was a British monk whose teaching was completely antithetical to that which Augustine articulated as the true and biblically-consistent anthropology. It has had a widespread influence in the church throughout the centuries since Pelagius was engaged in debate by Augustine in the fifth century. It reappeared in the so-called Remonstrant theology in the early seventeenth century, when it was countered by the vigorous defense of the biblical faith at the Synod of Dordt in 1618-19. At that time the defective doctrines of the Arminians were exposed in the Canons of Dordt which formalized what have become known as the "five points of Calvinism."[20] Pelagianism, or varying degrees of what have been referred to as semi-Pealgianism, tarnished the theology of the evangelical awakening in the eighteenth century. It marked the divergence between John Wesley and George Whitefield in England,[21] and it was exposed for its doctrinal fallacies by the prominent philosopher-theologian, Jonathan Edwards, in the United States.[22] We leave aside for

---

[20] The literature on that very important episode in the history of the church is copious. A valuable discussion is contained in Cunningham, *Historical Theology*, 2:373ff. The history of the Synod of Dordt and the content of the Canons of Dordt may be inspected in Joel R. Beeke and Sinclair B. Ferguson, *Reformed Confessions Harmonized* (Grand Rapids: Baker Books, 1999).

[21] The Wesley-Whitefield divergence is reported in Arnold Dallimore's two-volume biography, *George Whitefield: The Life and Times of the Great Evangelist of the Eighteenth-Century Revival* (Edinburgh: Banner of Truth, 1970 and 1979). See 1:307-19, 451-2.

[22] Jonathan Edwards' *An Inquiry into ... [the] Freedom of the Will* (Morgan, PA.: Soli Deo Gloria Publications, 1996), which established Edwards' reputation as foremost among American philosophers, was

the present the extent to which the essence of Pelagianism is enshrined in the Roman Catholic theology and that of Thomas Aquinas that has heavily influenced the Catholic system of doctrine. But varying forms and degrees of semi-Pelagianism, with its emphasis on the freedom and competence of the unregenerate will, continue to inform expressions of present-day evangelicalism.

The question that comes to principal focus, so far as our present argument is concerned, is that of what is to be understood as the capacity and competence of the human faculty of the will as it exists after, and as a result of, Adam's fall. The more fully-developed Reformed theology concludes that at the Fall all of the faculties of the soul were affected and disabled, in the respect that they were hence no longer characterized by the ability and capacity to perform the function and discharge the offices that were mandated to our first parents. We speak, as a result, of the total depravity of the faculties of the soul that resulted from the Fall. The mind, or the intellectual faculty, was darkened in that it was blinded by the devil to whom Adam had capitulated in his damning decision and assumption of autonomy. "The god of this world hath blinded the minds of them which believe not" (2 Cor. 4:4). Henceforth, "the wickedness of man was great in the earth, and every imagination of his heart was only evil continually" (Gen. 6:5). "The heart is deceitful above all

---

written for the explicit purpose of contradicting the Arminian doctrine. A recent scholar, Conrad Cherry, observes judiciously in his *The Theology of Jonathan Edwards: A Reappraisal* (Bloomington: Indiana University Press, 1990), that "the essay *Freedom of the Will* was intended to reduce the arguments of the Arminians to absurdity" op. cit., 160. See also Douglas Vickers, *Christian Confession and the Crackling Thorn: The Imperatives of Faith in an Age of Unbelief* (Grand Rapids: Reformation Heritage Books, 2004), 59. A definitive response to the Arminian doctrine, so far as it bears on the possibility and process of salvation, is contained in the seventeenth-century work of John Owen, *The Death of Death in the Death of Christ* (London: Banner of Truth, 1959).

things, and desperately wicked; who can know it?" (Jer. 17:9). The emotional faculty was depraved to the extent that unregenerate persons, having surrendered their pristine love of God, are now "haters of God" (Rom. 1:30). And the will, or the volitional faculty, is now weakened to the extent that the natural man is now "the servant [slave] of sin" (John 8:34).[23] The disabilities that are thus involved mean and imply that "the natural man receiveth not the things of the Spirit of God; for they are foolishness unto him; neither can he know them, because they are spiritually discerned" (1 Cor. 2:14). Such is the sorry condition to which the Fall reduced mankind. As to man's competence and ability to turn from sin to God, the realities are that at the Fall man lost his free will.

The Pelagian claims saw things vastly differently. Adolf Harnack, commenting on "the principles of the Pelagian doctrine," has rightly observed that "it has made its appearance in a subtle form again and again."[24] Harnack notes in relation to the Pelagian scheme that it claims that "Everything that God has created is good, therefore also the creature, the law and free-will... accordingly there can exist no *peccata naturalia* [sin as a matter of nature], only *peccata per accidens*. Human nature can be modified only incidentally. The most important and best endowment of this nature is free-will."[25] Harnack continues in his description of the Pelagian scheme, "Man is able to resist every sin, therefore he must do so.... Sin always remains an affair of the will and each is punished only for his own sin. All men stand in the condition of Adam before his fall."[26]

It is clear that the Pelagian scheme, against which

---

[23] The enslavement of the will to sin is explored in Martin Luther's reply to Erasmus in his *The Bondage of the Will*, trans. J. I. Packer and O. R. Johnston (Westwood, N.J.: Fleming Revell, 1957).
[24] Adolf Harnack, *Outlines of the History of Dogma*, trans. E. K. Mitchell (Boston: Beacon Press, 1957), 368-69.
[25] Ibid., 369.
[26] Ibid., 370.

Augustine argued vehemently, completely misrepresents the biblical doctrine of the Fall. For Pelagius, the will did not suffer damage at the Fall, no fallen nature has been transmitted as a result of the Fall, and every man is able by the exercise of his free will to do what is good as God mandates the good. The further implication, as to its evangelical import, is that every man is able to turn to God at will, and that individual salvation is therefore a matter purely of individual decision and competence. That implies that man is effectively sovereign in his own salvation. In his larger multi-volume work on the *History of Dogma* Harnack refers to the Pelagian doctrine as stated at the Synod of Carthage in the year 418 as claiming that "man can be without sin and can keep the divine commands easily if he will."[27]

What is at issue in the Pelagian-Augustinian controversy can be put by asking what is to be understood, on the basis of the biblical data, as to the process and effectiveness of salvation. If it is said, as is implicit in the Pelagian view, that one's salvation is altogether dependent on one's own sovereign power and action of choice, then salvation is an *autosoterism*. By that it is being said that man saves himself. He is himself sovereign in that crucial act and decision. If, however, it were said that man in his natural state is damaged in his faculties to the degree that he needs the assistance of divine grace, then it would be implied that salvation is a process of *synergism*. Salvation is then a matter of a synergistic cooperation between God and man. It is in that form that semi-Pelagianism has become current in many expressions of evangelicalism. It amounts to the claim that God has done his part in making salvation available to all men by reason of the death of his Son, and that now it is left to man to do his part.

---

[27] Adolf Harnack, *History of Dogma*, 7 vols., trans. James Millar (New York: Dover, 1951), 5:175, quoted in R. C. Sproul, *Faith Alone: The Evangelical Doctrine of Justification* (Grand Rapids: Baker Books, 1995), 136.

The possibility of one's salvation then turns on an individual's willingness to express again his sovereign decision to accept, rather than reject, the offer of salvation. In that case, God is seen as standing by, essentially a helpless bystander, waiting to observe the outcome. But the biblical doctrine as it has come to its full expression in the Reformation theology is that salvation is not, in the preceding sense, an *autosoterism*, and neither is it a human-divine *synergism*. Rather, salvation is a divine *monergism*. Salvation is entirely a work and a result of divine grace. "By grace are ye saved through faith," the apostle argued to the Ephesians, "and that not of yourselves; it is the gift of God" (Eph. 2:8).

In a highly significance sense, Pelagius stood for a *human monergism*, while Augustine argued biblically for a *divine monergism*.[28] Cunningham observed that "Augustine laboured for about twenty years, with all the powers of his mind, and with unwearied zeal and assiduity, in opposition to the errors of Pelagius; writing many books on the subject ... and exerting his influence in every other way to prevent the spread of the heresy. The Lord was pleased to call him to his rest in the year 430 ... without affording him the satisfaction of witnessing the triumph of sound doctrine, and the condemnation of its opponents in the General Council of Ephesus [in 431]."[29] The Pelagian theology has been treated at length by Turretin, who comments on the state of the faculty of the will by observing that "the question returns to this – whether unregenerate man still has such strength of free will as to be indifferent to good and evil and is able not to sin without the grace of regeneration. The adversaries affirm; we deny." Turretin continues, "Here we have as opponents the old and new Pelagians (who place the idol of free will in the citadel) and to make men free, make them sacrilegious."[30]

---

[28] See Schaff, *History*, 3:786.
[29] Cunningham, *Historical Theology*, 1:329.
[30] Turretin, *Elenctic Theology*, 1:669.

It can be noted in this connection, finally, that Pelagianism, by reason of its insistence on the undamaged capacity of the will and the varying forms in which it has reappeared in semi-Pelagianism, has pointed the way to the view that faith is either supplemented by, or stands alone without the need of, grace, and that it exists simply in individual obedience. That has led at different times in the history of the church to doctrines of "new obedience" or "neonomianism" or to a viewpoint that sees the religious relation to God as existing principally in moral actions.[31] It has led also to a confusion as to the place of the good works of the Christian in his justification and his sanctification. In its neonomian form it gave rise to considerable debate and theological agitation in eighteenth-century England, and called forth the response of Edward Fisher in his *The Marrow of Modern Divinity* which, history records, had an extensive influence in Scotland at that time.[32] More recently, similar doctrinal difficulties have appeared in the evangelical literature, instanced, for example, by the work of Norman Shepherd, and have given rise to considerable debate in Reformed and evangelical churches.[33] But a clear view of the biblical doctrines of the status of man and his faculties as a result of the Fall, of sin and the consequent relevance of grace, of forensic justification and sanctification,

---

[31] Some aspects of this tendency were addressed in the nineteenth-century work of Herman Bavinck, *Reformed Dogmatics, Volume 1: Prolegomena* (Grand Rapids: Baker Academic, 2003), 258.

[32] Edward Fisher, *The Marrow of Modern Divinity*, with notes by Thomas Boston (Scarsdale, N.Y.: Westminster Discount Book Service, n.d.). The Marrow controversy is discussed in John Macleod, *Scottish Theology: In relation to church history since the Reformation* (Edinburgh: Banner of Truth, 1974), 139ff.

[33] See Norman Shepherd, *The Call of Grace: How the Covenant Illuminates Salvation and Evangelism* (Phillipsburg: P&R, 2000), and a summing up of a relevant doctrinal and ecclesiastical debate in O. Palmer Robertson, *The Current Justification Controversy* (Unicoi, Tennessee: The Trinity Foundation, 2003). See also Vickers, *Christian Confession*, 150-51.

and of the place of Christian obedience make confusion in these important respects unnecessary. The great Dutch theologian, Herman Witsius, writing in the late seventeenth century, clarified the relevant issues and put to rest the misunderstandings of doctrine, and he refuted completely the errors that have reemerged in more recent times.[34]

Anselm and the doctrine of the atonement

Anselm, who served as Archbishop of Canterbury from 1093 until his death in 1109 at the age of 75, has been referred to by one reliable historian as "one of the ablest and purest men of the mediaeval church.... He was the most original thinker the Church had seen since the days of Augustine."[35] And another has concluded that "It is remarkable that the bursting forth of a new spirit of inquiry, the dawning of a new era after five hundred years of stagnation and darkness, should have commenced with the sudden appearance of a man of such remarkable depth, clearness, and living piety, as that of Anselm."[36] Shedd observes that "in the very opening of a new era ... we find a view of the work of Christ, decidedly in advance of the best soteriology of the Patristic age, and agreeing substantially with that of the Reformation."[37] It is Anselm's soteriology, his contribution to the doctrine of the atonement of Christ, that is of immediate interest.

Anselm is famously remembered for two main contributions. First, he developed what has become known as the ontological proof of the existence of God; and second, his doctrine of the necessity and significance of the death of

---

[34] Witsius, *Economy of the Covenants*, 1:410-11.
[35] Schaff, *History*, 5:598.
[36] Shedd, *History*, 2:273. Shedd's *History* (first edition 1863), along with his three volume *Dogmatic Theology* (1888), (Grand Rapids: Zondervan, n.d.), remains a valuable treatment of the main movements in theological doctrinal development.
[37] Idem, 2:273-74.

Christ presented in clear terms what has since been referred to as the satisfaction theory or explanation of the atonement. We comment only briefly on the first of these contributions.

The ontological proof of the existence of God has occupied philosophers since Anselm's first statement of it and continues to be a matter of lively dispute. The essence of Anselm's statement is that it is possible to conceive of a being "than which no greater can be thought,"[38] and, further, that the being which is so conceived must necessarily exist in reality. Anselm's argument, as translated from his own words, claims that "Therefore, if that than which nothing greater can be conceived exists *in the understanding alone*, the very being than which nothing greater can be conceived is one than which a greater *can* be conceived. But obviously this is impossible. Hence there is no doubt that there exists a being than which nothing greater can be conceived, and it exists *both in understanding and reality.*"[39]

It is well-known in the philosophic literature that an opponent of Anselm on this point, Gaunilo, responded that it was not possible, as Anselm had claimed, to argue from the subjective conception of such a being as was contemplated to his, or its, objective existence in reality. The real existence of a thing must first be established, Gaunilo argued, before anything can be predicated of it. The ontological proof was again formulated by Descartes at the beginning of modern philosophy in the seventeenth century,[40] and in due course it

---

[38] The argument was set forth in Anselm's *Monologium* or *Soliloquy* and later stated in more complete form in his *Proslogium* or *Allocation*. The "proof" is discussed in Schaff, *History*, 5:601f., and, for a modern view, in Robert L. Reymond, *A New Systematic Theology of the Christian Faith* (Nashville: Thomas Nelson, 1998), 132ff.

[39] Cited in Reymond, op. cit., 132, italics added.

[40] Rene Descartes, *Discourse on Method and the Meditations*, various editions. The ontological proof argument, grounded for Descartes in his "idea of a perfect being," appears in Part IV on the *Discourse on Reason*.

attracted, most notably at the hands of the late-Enlightenment philosopher, Immanuel Kant, the same objection as Gaunilo had stated. It is generally agreed that Anselm's argument fails by reason that existence cannot be taken to be a predicate in the sense he intended.

It might be noted that a contemporary apologist, R. C. Sproul, has claimed to have remedied Anselm's logically defective argument. He has argued that the "proof" of God's existence is completed as follows. "When one adds the simple observation that the necessary proof of anything is the inability to think of its nonexistence, this establishes the necessary existence of the perfect being.... When one adds that Anselm's being, than which none greater can be conceived, cannot be thought not to exist, he has proven the actual necessary real existence of that being." Sproul based his argument on the proposition that "We cannot think of the nonexistence of perfect, necessary being."[41] It is by no means clear, however, that Sproul's argument warrants universal acceptance as a logical demonstration. But we have noted Anselm's argument at this point for two reasons.

First, if Anselm's argument does have to be seen as logically defective for the reason indicated, it nevertheless contains, or is grounded on, a significant truth. That is that the sensibility of the being and the existence of God does exist as an ineradicable intuition in the human mind. There is created in the human consciousness both a *sensus deitatis*, a sense of God, and a *semen religionis*, a seed of religion from which there is no escape. "The fool hath said in his heart, There is no God" (Ps. 14:1). The apostle Paul argued forcibly in the first chapter of his letter to the Romans that as to the true state of the human person, "when they knew God ... they changed the

---

[41] R. C. Sproul, Arthur Lindsley, and John Gerstner, *Classical Apologetics: A Rational Defense of the Christian Faith and a Critique of Presuppositional Apologetics* (Grand Rapids: Zondervan, 1984), 102-103.

truth of God into a lie, and worshipped and served the creature more than the Creator" (Rom. 1:21-25), and they "held in unrighteousness," or "suppressed," the truth that was clearly displayed in their consciousness (Rom. 1:18).

Secondly, Anselm's argument, by reason that it is presented in the context of a prayerful cry to God, attests the high piety of the man, his devotion to truth and righteousness, and his single-minded concern for the glory of God. His extensive correspondence betrays his sincere pastoral interest. Schaff observes that "He was revered as a saint before his official canonization in 1494."[42] The recognition of those characteristics and the spiritual insight they attest bring to heightened significance Anselm's argument regarding the satisfaction that Christ effected in his atonement.

Anselm's discussion of the atonement is presented in his *Cur Deus homo*, "Why God became Man," and in this, Schaff comments, "a new chapter opens in the development of the doctrine of the atonement."[43] Anselm begins his discussion by arguing, first, for the *necessity* of the coming of Christ and his atonement. The ensuing argument anticipates what is now held as biblically-consistent doctrine in the best Reformed tradition. Man has sinned against God, in that he has withheld from God the obedience and honor due to him. He has thereby acquired the guilt of indebtedness to God. If, however, God were simply to declare that debt wiped away by his mercy and love and compassion, he would be violating his own justice. God's honor must be restored to him, and that must be done in such a manner that a double satisfaction for the debt that man incurs must be paid. That is because, firstly, the debt accrues by reason of past sins, and secondly, because the law of God must be honored by future obedience. If only the debt for past sin was paid, then man would still be left to bear the liability for his future sins which would inevitably occur. But man in

---

[42] Schaff, *History*, 5:600.
[43] Schaff, ibid., 5:604.

the state in which he now exists is a sinner, and it is therefore impossible for him to discharge that double obligation. Anselm reaches the conclusion that it was necessary that God should himself satisfy his own requirements of justice in the matter. Taking his argument to the very heart of what he conceived of as the nature of God, Anselm saw that only God could provide his own required satisfaction. At the same time, Anselm saw that it was necessary that *man* should render the satisfaction, because otherwise it would not be a satisfaction for *man's* sin. It followed clearly, then, that the required satisfaction must be provided by one who was both God and man. The satisfaction must be made by incarnate deity.[44]

It would be a mistake to conclude that Anselm, in his remarkably clear and advanced statement of doctrine, has said all that is to be said on the subject of our Lord's substitutionary atonement. The development of doctrine at and after the sixteenth-century Reformation added necessary dimensions to the statement and clarification of the biblical revelation. Issues of Christology, the doctrinal locus having to do with the Person of Christ, and of soteriology, the doctrine of the redemption that Christ accomplished, have benefited from expansion in the literature already referred to.

Nor is it correct to say that the remarkable doctrinal advance due to Anselm influenced the church from his time on, in the sense that his achievement permanently affected and influenced the church's doctrinal stance. It has been remarked that if that had been so, then the rediscovery of the doctrine of justification by faith that is due to Luther and the Reformation achievement would not have been necessary.[45]

It can at the same time be said, however, that the aspects of the development of doctrine that we have inspected address the very foundation of what became in due course a fully-

---

[44] See the discussion and summary of Anselm's doctrine in Shedd, *History*, and Schaff, *History*.
[45] See Shedd, *History*, 2:285.

developed Reformed theology. First, Athanasius' defense of the truth of the biblical revelation against the claims of Arius directs us to the fuller consideration of the being of the Godhead and the deity of the Son, or his autotheotic nature. Second, in doing so, it enables us to see the fuller meaning of Anselm's claim that God himself, in the Person of his Son, entered into historical time to redeem us from the entailment of the sin into which Adam's dereliction had cast us. And third, the state of sin that occasions the disabilities to which Anselm drew attention and emphasized strongly is clarified by the argument of Augustine in which he rejected Pelagius' claim for human free will. These early theological conclusions establish the critical doctrinal loci in terms of which the meaning of both the human condition and the possibility of its rescue are to be explored. The Reformation theology stands on the achievements of Athanasius, Augustine, and Anselm. The fuller respects in which that is so warrant careful investigation, and some of the principal relations and conclusions will emerge in the chapters that follow.

The way ahead

With the benefit of what has now been adduced from the development of theological doctrine we return to the question raised at the beginning. What is to be understood as describing the contemporary human condition? What is the indictment that the biblical revelation raises against it? And what, in the light of our diagnosis, is to be said as to the possibility and the means of its rescue and relief?

In short, the human condition is what it is because all mankind stands by nature under the bequest of Adam's fall. We have noted the Westminster catechists' conclusion that all mankind, descending from Adam by ordinary generation, sinned in him and fell with him. The catechism goes on to say, observing on the sinfulness and the misery of the state that resulted, that "the sinfulness of that estate whereinto man fell, consists in the guilt of Adam's first sin, the want of original righteousness, and the corruption of his whole nature, which is commonly called original sin, together with all actual transgressions which proceed from it."[46] And "All mankind, by their fall, lost communion with God, are under his wrath and curse, and so made liable to all miseries in this life, to death itself, and to the pains of hell forever."[47] The contemporary condition is what it is because we have turned our backs on the obligation we have sustained by reason that we are the creatures of a Creator-God. We stand in the condition we do because we now have no recognition of the righteousness of the law of life that God has given for our rule and guidance.

In the chapters that follow that condition will be subject to more detailed examination and our argument will proceed as follows. In the next chapter we shall look in some depth at the meaning and significance of the covenant that God established with our first parents, commonly referred to as the covenant of creation or the covenant of works. In terms of that covenant man's delegated offices were clearly mandated and his obligations to God were articulated and established. It will emerge that the state of sin, as that has already been referred to as a result of Adam's fall, amounted to a repudiation of covenantal obligations, and ever since that has driven to the heart of the explanation of the condition of man.

It will be necessary then to explore at more length the reality that at the Fall, as Augustine argued in response to Pelagius, man lost his free will. The terms of that conclusion will be explored in such a way as to confront the question of the relation between the divine sovereignty of God and human responsibility. Mystery exists, of course, in that relation, as mystery exists at the end of every doctrine of the Christian faith. But an attempt will be made to address the important question as to precisely where, and why, the mystery resides.

---

[46] Westminster Shorter Catechism, Question 18.
[47] Ibid., Question 19.

It will be concluded that there is no need for the Christian confession to be embarrassed by the admission of mystery. For while mystery exists for man, no mystery exists for God.

At that point, and taking account, as Athanasius saw it, of the realities of the divine Personhood of the Son of God who came into the world for our redemption, and holding to the necessity of his coming to provide a satisfaction for our sin as Anselm alerted us to see, we shall consider further the possibility and the accomplishment of redemption. That very possibility lies in that fact that not only do we know God, but we know him as a decreeing God. Redemption turns on the eternal decree that issued from the council of the Godhead before the foundation of the world.

The Second Person of the Godhead came into the world as Jesus Christ to save his people from their sins. That he did so lies at the heart of the good news of the gospel. But beyond the precise intention and accomplishment of salvation lies the wider reality of what we shall refer to as the cosmic significance of Christ. His present rule over all things, his heavenly High Priestly session, and the prospect of his eternal reign are integral to that wider reality.

Those whom Christ redeemed are introduced to a new solidarity. The old solidarity in Adam has been replaced by a solidarity in Christ. The union that is thereby established with their redeemer, a vital, organic, spiritual, and indissoluble union, comes to expression in the believers' entrance into the church in its visible form. Christ rules as Head of his church, and the implications that follow, not only for the reality of the church invisible, but for the church visible and militant as it exists in this world, will be explored.

Finally, the necessity and the meaning of the response that naturally wells up in the heart and life of the Christian person will come into view. The meaning will be explored of the fact that by reason of his redemption by the vicarious suffering and work of Christ, all of the Christian's life is to be lived under the imperative of obedience to the law of God.

That imperative, lived out in the integrity, but in the inevitable imperfection, of the Christian endeavor, will be seen to be addressed in all things to the glory of God.

Chapter 2

The Prelapsarian Covenant

The diagnosis of the contemporary condition turns, the preceding chapter has concluded, on the understanding of two biblically-stated realities. First, man came from the hands of his Creator in a condition of holiness and righteousness and in that pristine state he was subject to certain mandates and obligations to God. Second, our first parents did not continue in the state in which they were created. The probation in which they had been placed was terminated by their repudiation of their covenantal obligations. All those descending from Adam by ordinary generation henceforth lived in a state of sin, subject to enslavement to sin. The faculties of soul were depraved, and there was no longer any fear of God before their eyes. The primeval love of God was replaced by a hatred of God that emanated from the disabilities that characterized the intellectual, emotional, and volitional faculties.

We look now at more length at the initial covenantal relation in which our first parents were established. Consideration is thereby given to the mandates to which they were subjected and to the respects in which the disabilities inherent in their Fall came to expression. The results of the Fall continue to inform the status of human personhood. Secondly, the clarification of the status of personhood will bring to clearer focus the meaning of the coming into the world of the Son of God as the redeemer who would save his people from their sins (Matt. 1:21). We shall speak, then, of the covenant of works that God initially established with our first parents at their creation, and also, in the light of their dereliction, the coming of a substitute redeemer. That will examine what doctrinal theology has considered under the heading of soteriology, or the subject of what determines and explains the salvation of the sinners whom Christ came to redeem.

Bringing together the doctrinal rubric of soteriology and that of the covenant of works addresses a relation that is critical to understanding redemption's process. For it brings to prominence two questions, the answers to which drive to the heart of the biblical-Reformation doctrine of the design and accomplishment of redemption. First, are we to say, on the grounds of the biblical data, that God established with our first parents what Reformation theology has articulated as a covenant of works, that in doing so he bound himself to promises of potential benediction and malediction, and that he bound Adam to certain mandates, responsibilities, and obligations? And second, are we to say that our eternal security, or in other words the believer's title to heaven, is grounded in the satisfaction of the obligations that were first set forth in the covenant of works? Our answers to both those questions are in the affirmative.

It will establish the perspective from which to consider these questions to note at the outset that we are concerned with the covenant that God made with Adam in his prelapsarian state. The subsequent Sinaitic covenant that God made with Moses has frequently been referred to as a covenant of works. But that is not appropriate terminology, as the Mosaic administration is properly to be seen and understood as a form of God's administration of the covenant of grace. We shall refer below to a work by Edward Fisher, *The Marrow of Modern Divinity*, that was influential in eighteenth-century Scotland. That work speaks of "the moral law [as given to Moses] as a covenant of works," reflecting the language of the Westminster Larger Catechism, Question 97. But it will be noted that Fisher, in joining the concepts of the moral law and the covenant of works, does so by maintaining that the Ten Commandments given to Moses were, in effect, already communicated to Adam in his prelapsarian state. Mark W. Karlberg has observed judiciously that "The Mosaic Covenant is to be viewed *in some sense* as a covenant of works. This has been the conviction of the vast majority of Reformed theologians in the early history of federalism."[1] We shall discuss also in several contexts what we have referred to as a "works principle."[2] That "principle" was present in the Mosaic system, as in Adam's initial state, but it did not there amount to a covenant of works which could be construed to have salvific competence. In the Mosaic state it meant that God did reward with blessing human works of obedience. The grounds on which the curses and blessings in Deuteronomy 27 and 28 are projected are eloquent on the point. It is the operation of a works principle in the Mosaic administration and the history of the Israelitish kingdom that accounts for the Babylonian captivity and the ultimate desolation of Jerusalem.

John Murray has provided a brief history of the development of the doctrine of the covenant of works,[3] but Murray himself, contrary to the position we shall take, doubts the

---

[1] Mark W. Karlberg, "Reformed Interpretation of the Mosaic Covenant," *Westminster Theological Journal*, Fall 1980, 3. See ibid. 54 and chapter 3 below for Karlberg's comment on the "works principle."

[2] A discussion of that "principle" appears in Meredith Kline's "Covenant Theology under Attack," *New Horizons* (February, 1994), 3-5, also http://www.opc.org/new_horizons/Kline_cov_theo.html, 1-5.

[3] John Murray, "Covenant Theology," in *Collected Writings of John Murray* (Edinburgh: Banner of Truth, 4 vols., 1976-1982), 4:217-22.

appropriateness of construing God's relations with Adam as a covenant of works. It is worthy of note that while the Westminster Confession of Faith and the Savoy Declaration of Faith contain reference to a covenant of works, no such reference appears explicitly in the Belgic Confession, the Heidelberg Catechism, or the Canons of Dort. But the doctrine may be implicit in, for example, the Belgic Confession, Articles 14 and 15, and the Canons of Dort, III-IV.[4]

The doctrine of the covenant of works, however, has lately fallen on hard times. Within the evangelical theological community a twofold claim has been made. First, it has long been a misunderstanding, it is now being said, that the pristine Creator-creature relation contained within its compass a divine commitment to promises such as those already stated, and that God thereby entered into a sworn obligation to his creature. And second, it is claimed, as a result, that the designation of the "covenant of works" should be deleted from the theological vocabulary.[5]

The Covenant of Works

The conclusion of our argument is implicit in what has already been said. The believer's title to heaven is grounded in the satisfaction of the obligations set forth in the covenant of works. That is so in the important respect that the meaning of

---

[4] See the extended discussion in Beeke and Ferguson, *Reformed Confessions Harmonized*, 52-53.

[5] Our construction of God's pristine relation with Adam as a covenant of works, contra some objections referred to above, is supported by authors in the Reformed tradition. Charles Hodge speaks at length of the "Covenant of Works" in his *Systematic Theology* (London: Thomas Nelson, 3 vols., 1873), 2:117ff., and at ibid. 364 he observes that "Had he [Adam] retained his integrity he would have merited the promised blessing." See A. A. Hodge, *Outlines of Theology* (Edinburgh: Banner of Truth, 1972), 309ff. L. Berkhof discusses the relevant doctrine at length in his widely-used and influential *Systematic Theology* (Grand Rapids: Eerdmans, 1939), 211ff.

the coming into the world of the blessed Second Person of the Godhead turns on that very condition. The Son of God and the Savior of men came that he might fulfill, on behalf of the people whom the Father gave him to redeem, the obligations they had sustained by reason of God's initial covenant with them in Adam, but which, by virtue of their dereliction and sin, remained unfulfilled. Christ came to do for his people what they were obligated to do but could not do for themselves. It is in that respect that he was their Substitute, and that the benefits of his obedience was placed to their account.

The biblical data are eloquent and may be summarized briefly. Five statements from the Genesis record capsule the relevant issues and will lay the background for subsequent discussion. First, "God said, 'Let us make man in our image, after our likeness'" (Gen. 1:26). The holiness that characterized Adam's original condition was inherent in the fact that in his creaturehood and derivative personhood he imaged his Creator. But that holiness would be sustained only on the grounds of his continued covenantal obedience.[6]

Second, "God said ... let them have dominion ..." (Gen. 1:26-28). Adam's status in which he enjoyed derivative dominion carried with it clearly implied vicegerent responsibilities and obligations. It is not to be understood that our first parents' prerogative of dominion and rule constituted an aspect of the image of God in which they were established. That prerogative is to be seen, rather, as referable to a delegated function they were obligated to perform by reason that they were creatively constituted as the image of God.[7]

---

[6] The meaning of the fact that man was created as the image of God has been explored at length in Vickers, *Christian Confession and the Crackling Thorn*, chap. 3. The fact that man *is* the image of God, not simply that he *bears* the image of God, establishes and underlines the covenantal obligations we are now addressing.

[7] Turretin, *Elenctic Theology,* 1:469, and Herman Bavinck, *In the Beginning* (Grand Rapids: Baker, 1999), 81, suggest that Adam's prerogative of rule and dominion is to be understood as an aspect of the

Third, the Genesis record clearly states the terms of Adam's probation and the implicit promises of benediction and malediction that God addressed to him. "Of the tree of the knowledge of good and evil, thou shalt not eat of it; for in the day that thou eatest thereof thou shalt surely die" (Gen. 2:17). The outcome of our first parents' probation is all too clear. But what, it is to be asked, was the sin that constituted their dereliction? Precisely, of course, it was their eating the forbidden fruit.[8] But behind that action lay the process of reasoning that led to their damning assumption of autonomy from God their Creator. True, the statement that God had made to them was clear and clearly understandable. But the counter-statement of the tempter was also, they assumed, worthy of consideration. Wisdom, as they saw it, may lie in the adoption of the tempter's proposal. The case was soon settled. Confronting the statements of both God and the tempter, our parents were not paralyzed by indecision. They themselves, in a false assumption of autonomy and independence, would decide the issue and choose between the competing claims. Thus there entered into apostate conception and experience the claim of autonomy that has characterized the human condition ever since.[9] But the sin that terminated their probation consisted in the fact that in the decision and action our first parents took they repudiated their covenantal obligations. That, in its final significance and import, is the meaning of sin. Sin is a repudiation of covenantal obligations.

---

image of God. For the view we have taken see Murray, *Collected Writings*, 2:41. John Owen makes the distinction that "man was ... God's image ... and was taught to have dominion," *Biblical Theology*, trans. S.P. Westcott (Pittsburg, PA: Soli Deo Gloria, 1994), 24.

[8] Westminster Shorter Catechism, Question 15.

[9] For a discussion of the historical development of the assumption of the autonomy of human thought, leading to its definitive statement by Immanuel Kant at the conclusion of the Enlightenment at the turn from the eighteenth to the nineteenth century, see Douglas Vickers, *The Fracture of Faith: Recovering Belief of the Gospel in a Postmodern World* (Fearn, Scotland: Christian Focus Publications, 2000), chap. 2.

We stay for a moment with the terms of God's probationary directive. It contained promises of both benediction and malediction. The promise of death upon disobedience was explicit and direct. But two things are clear from the Scriptural record. First, when it is seen that all of God's relations with man are to be understood and interpreted as covenantal relations, those relations carry with them the alternative promises of blessing and curse. Blessing and benediction in the event of covenantal obedience, and curse and malediction in the event of disobedience, are inherent in all aspects of the Creator-creature covenantal relations. The Old Testamental data are replete to that effect. The terms and procedures of the covenant with Abraham, for example (Gen. 15:9ff.), convey within them the promise of potential curse. That is clarified by reason, first, of Abraham's submission to the blood sign of circumcision that constituted the divinely stated initiatory rite, where the blood sign portended death in the event of failure to honor the terms of the covenant as it had been instituted.[10] It is instanced also by God's passing between the parts of the dismembered animals. For in his passing between the animal parts, God swore his own oath of faithfulness. Hebrews 6:17 states that "God ... confirmed it by an oath." If he should not be faithful to his promise, God was there stating, then let him not be God. Of immediate relevance, however, is the fact that in the initial Adamic covenant the same realities applied. Blessing would follow obedience and curse would ensue from disobedience. In that context it is to be seen that God's oath of faithfulness is present in the initial probationary directive. So insistent should that be for our doctrinal construction that its terms may be noted more fully.

---

[10] For a discussion of the importance and doctrinal relevance of the promises of benediction and malediction inherent in the divine covenants see Meredith G. Kline, *By Oath Consigned: A Reinterpretation of the Covenant Signs of Circumcision and Baptism* (Grand Rapids: Eerdmans, 1968).

The upshot of what is at issue can be stated briefly and pointedly. In the Adamic covenant, given its terms as indicated, God placed himself under an unalterable obligation to Adam, his creature. That, in short, is the issue that is to be grasped if the dimensions and the significance of the covenant of works are to be adequately understood. Startling as it may appear to our unpracticed ears, there came into effect at that point a "works principle," whereby God obligated himself to reward Adam on the grounds of his work of obedience to the covenantal obligations that were then articulated. That was so in the respect that God swore to be faithful to the promise of blessing and life in response to Adam's faithful execution of the mandates entrusted to him. Or to put the issue in other terms, God, having made a conditional promise of life to Adam, thereby placed himself under obligation to the demands of his own eternally holy character and righteousness.[11] The implications of that defining statement direct us not only, as has been said, to preserving in doctrinal terms and substance the covenant of works, but to the necessity also of maintaining corresponding language in our theological

---

[11] The concept of the "works principle" has long been understood as an essential part of God's covenantal arrangements with man, and the deviation from it has only recently become a part of the dissent from the covenant of works that we shall refer to below. Witsius has made the point in his comment that "God has, by his promises, made himself a debtor to man. Or, to speak in a manner more becoming God, he was pleased to make his performing his promises, a debt to himself, to his goodness, justice, and veracity," *Economy of the Covenants*, 1:48; and "Such a perfect observance of the laws of the covenant, quite to the period which God had fixed for probation, had given man a right to the reward ... from God's ... engagement, which was no ways unbecoming him to enter into," idem, 70. The same point regarding God's covenantal engagement to reward Adam's works of obedience is stated in Thomas Boston's notes to Fisher's *Marrow of Modern Divinity*, "After man was created ... a threatening of eternal death in the case of disobedience, had also a promise of eternal life annexed to it in the case of obedience; in virtue of which he, having done his work, might thereupon plead and demand the reward of eternal life," op. cit., 26.

lexicon. In that initial Adamic covenant we are to see the real possibility of Adam's attaining the reward promised and, in harmonious relation, God's real promise and commitment to bestow that reward if Adam sustained his probation.

At the risk of needless repetition, but to keep before us the relevance of that to the whole range of soteriological issues, it is the works principle involved in the earlier Creator-creature relation that explains the redemptive mission of our Lord in this world. He not only bore the penalty of our sin, but he completed for us the obligation of works of obedience in relation to which we were in dereliction. He did for us what we were obligated to do, but were unable to do, for ourselves.

Consider, to stay with that reality a little further, God's initial probationary directive. We turn now to the implicit promise it contained of benediction and life. The significance of that promise is clear from the outcome that followed the obedience of Christ. "When all was sin and shame," the hymn writer, John Henry Newman, has said, "a Second Adam to the fight and to the rescue came." That is precisely what is at issue. The Second Adam earned by his obedience the reward that the first Adam had forfeited (Rom. 5:19). The Second Adam fulfilled in human nature the hitherto unfulfilled obligations to which human nature was exposed. And in Christ, human nature was rewarded by its elevation to the right hand of the Father. That culmination constituted, in turn, the guarantee that all those whom Christ redeemed, again by his comprehensive obedience (Rom. 5:19), would reign with him in their own redeemed human nature and would share the reward that comes from the covenantal obedience he demonstrated on their behalf.

The fourth of the statements we have in view from the Genesis record is the familiar, but still indistinct, promise of the coming of a redeemer to interrupt and do away with the entailment of sin (Gen. 3:15). That promise, that a redeemer would come in the same, but sinless, human nature that had fallen into sin, was subject to progressive clarification and particularization in the Old Testament record. In due time (Gal. 4:4), our Lord came, as the antitype of all of the anticipatory types that preceded and pointed to him, to fulfill the promise and to be our redeemer.

Fifth, the Genesis record discloses that for Adam the *summum bonum* was that God walked with him "in the garden in the cool of the day" (Gen. 3:8). Though that Scriptural statement is made in the context of Adam's postlapsarian confrontation with God, such a privilege of communication and communion was clearly an essential aspect of the prelapsarian Creator-creature relation. For while, in his initial coming to created self-consciousness, Adam knew God, and in his state of inherent holiness he naturally loved and obeyed God, he was the recipient of further directives, mandates, and explanations of what was required of him.[12] Indeed, Adam received at that time God's directions as to the requirements of work, worship, the sabbath, and family and social relations that were subsequently inscripturated, in a form accommodated to our fallen condition, in the Decalogue as given to Moses.[13]

The Works of the Covenant

As we contemplate the terms of the covenant of works, the question naturally follows as to what is to be meant by the "works" on which the blessing, or alternatively the curse, of the covenant were suspended. It may be said that they contemplated and encompassed all that God had revealed to

---

[12] See Geerhardus Vos, *Biblical Theology: Old and New Testaments* (Grand Rapids: Eerdmans, 1948), 31 for a discussion of "Preredemptive Special Revelation."

[13] The same point was made at length in the eighteenth century Marrow controversy in Fisher's *The Marrow of Modern Divinity*, chap. 1, "The ten commandments ... though they were not written in tables of stone until the time of Moses, yet they were written in the table of man's heart in the time of Adam," op. cit., 30.

Adam as the requirements of righteous conformity to his law, including the moral law that was subsequently articulated in written form in the Ten Commandments. Those requirements are encapsuled again in God's subsequent statement to Abraham, "walk before me, and be thou perfect" (Gen. 17:1). But the five statements we have adduced from the Genesis record imply that the "works" of the covenant are contained in the mandate that Adam should discharge faithfully his delegated offices of prophet, priest, and king. A concentration on those Adamic offices enables us to bring into clearer focus, and to a sharper relevance than has generally been addressed in the literature, a relationship between the offices and obligations of Adam and those bestowed on Christ. In doing so, we may obtain also a clear view of both Adam's covenantal obligations and the meaning of the sin by which he fell.[14]

The rubric of the threefold office of prophet, priest, and king has become familiar to the Reformed theological tradition since Calvin elucidated the tripartite office of Christ in those terms.[15] Anticipating again our conclusion that Christ was the sinner's Substitute in fulfilling the previously unfulfilled obligations of the covenant of works, it follows that the tripartite office of Christ was what it was because he was the sinner's substitute prophet, his substitute priest, and his substitute king.[16] He came to discharge for us the obligations

---

[14] Adam's establishment in the mandated offices of prophet, priest, and king, with the covenantal obligations they implied, are discussed in Vickers, *Christian Confession*, 98-100.

[15] The doctrinal significance of the tripartite office of Christ as prophet, priest, and king received its principal impetus from Calvin, *Institutes of the Christian Religion*, 1:494, Book 2, chap. 15. That doctrinal motif was discussed further by Turretin in his important *Elenctic Theology*, 2:302-303. The doctrinal issues have been discussed in such modern treatises as Berkhof, *Systematic Theology*, 356f., and Reymond, *New Systematic Theology*, 623-24.

[16] Christ came into the world to be, as will be discussed at more length below, our prophet, priest, and king. But it is to recognize an important aspect of the biblical data to observe that man in his original constitu-

of the offices in relation to which we were disabled by virtue of our fall into sin.

Why, in short, were we, in the condition in which we existed as a result of our participation in Adam's fall (Rom. 5:12f.), in need of a Substitute? What, in other words, connoted the defects to which we were exposed by Adam's dereliction? The answer is that by reason of the darkness and deficiency to which we had fallen in Adam it was no longer possible for us to discharge the mandates of our office as prophet, priest, and king.

As has been seen from the reference to Adam's endowment of dominion status (Gen. 1:28), he was to exercise the office of prophet by investigating, understanding, explaining, and speaking back to God the meaning of the reality-environment in which, by virtue of his creation by the hand of God, he had come to self-consciousness. His beginning in that task is exemplified by his naming and explaining the animals (Gen. 2:19-20). The same Genesis record clarifies Adam's office as king, because he was commissioned to rule over all of created reality and "over every living thing."

In that connection the meaning becomes clear of the state of sin into which Adam had fallen and into which, by virtue of his representative and federal headship, he dragged us all. We have commented on the deliberative process that precipitated the disastrous action of our parents' eating the forbidden fruit. The essence of the meaning of sin that followed is that sin is to be understood, firstly and principally, as the state and

---

tion and status was charged with the prophetic, priestly, and kingly offices. Van Til has pointed in that direction in his understanding of the essentially explanatory aspect of Adam's prophetic office and in his statement that "The revelation of God was deposited in the whole of creation, but it was in the mind of man alone that this revelation was to come to self-conscious re-interpretation. Man was to be God's re-interpreter, that is, God's prophet on earth." *An Introduction to Systematic Theology* (Phillipsburg: Presbyterian and Reformed, 1974), 69-70.

condition into which all mankind had thereby fallen. Sin is not primarily a matter of action and behavior. And emphasized in that statement is the word "primarily." Of course it is true that an understanding of Adam's initial and prelapsarian condition requires it to be said that his sin was an ethical lapse and not a change in his being or metaphysical status. But while sin is ethical and not metaphysical, and while it is true that the actions of sin are such as outrage the holiness of God, those actions, completely contrary to the ethical mandates of the law of God as they are, are what they are by virtue of the state of blackness and darkness to which we had fallen. The Scriptural data are replete with explanation to that effect (2 Cor. 4:4; Eph. 2:1; 1 Cor 2:14; Jer. 17:9; John 8:44; Rom. 6:16; Luke 11:21).

The apostle John has elevated the righteousness of God in his explanation that "sin is the transgression of the law" (1 John 3:4), and the Westminster catechists have referred to sin as "any want of conformity unto, or transgression of, the law of God."[17] But both the apostle and the catechists made their defining statements against the fundamental realization that such law-breaking actions are precipitated by the blackened condition of soul into which we were cast by Adam's covenant-breaking act. The apostle's entire conception was fathered by his understanding of the lostness of the human soul apart from the redeeming grace of God set forth in Christ. He was therefore at pains to record the underlying fact that the wrath of God continues, it abides, it remains unremoved, on those who do not believe on the Son of God (John 3:36). And similarly, the authors of the Westminster Catechism were at pains to expose the underlying condition of sin that alone explained the sinner's God-dishonoring, law-breaking, covenant-repudiating actions. "Into what estate did the Fall bring mankind?" they ask. And having responded that "the Fall brought mankind into an estate of sin and misery," they

---

[17] *Westminster Shorter Catechism*, Question 14.

continued, "the sinfulness of that estate whereinto man fell consists in the guilt of Adam's first sin, the want of original righteousness, and the corruption of his whole nature, which is commonly called original sin, together with all actual transgressions which proceed from it."[18]

Three conclusions follow as to the meaning of sin. First, sin is in the first place a matter of state and condition, or as the catechists put it, a matter of "estate." Second, that condition involves the "corruption of [the sinner's] whole nature." And third, the actions of sin on the level of ethical conduct are what they are because they are the precipitate of that underlying condition of estrangement from God, "the loss of original righteousness." Adam's inability to act righteously followed from his loss of the original holiness that had characterized his condition as created in the image of God.

But we must sharpen further our grasp of the meaning of sin to clarify its relation to the covenant of works that we now have under discussion. We have said that the implication of Adam's fall into the state of sin was that he was no longer able to discharge his covenantal obligations and his obligated office of prophet. The essence of the prophetic office is that of explaining and understanding and dedicating back to God the meaning of the reality-environment in which Adam existed. In the darkness and ignorance that resulted, the deprivation and depravation in which the action of sin issued, Adam was no longer in possession of the categories of explanation that would have made the meaning of reality transparent. On the level of understanding and knowledge, that was the sorry condition that ensued.

From that condition two results follow. First, it is in that loss of prophetic office and competence that we discover the initial meaning of the effects of sin. For in his office as prophet Adam was obligated to unravel the meaning of the reality that God had spoken into existence, and he was to do

[18] Westminster Shorter Catechism, Questions 17, 18.

so by employing the terms of interpretation, the categories of understanding and explanation, that God had communicated to him. But that, lamentably, he was no longer able to do. God had spoken to Adam "in the garden in the cool of the day" (Gen. 3:8) and had communicated to him the necessary principles of the predication of meaning. But those Adam had surrendered by his damning claim of autonomy from his Creator, his false assertion of metaphysical, epistemological, and ethical autonomy.[19] Adam therefore sinned in that not only was he now in a state of defect in his loss of the true principles of predication and explanation, but because, also, in his God-hating condition (Rom. 1:30) he was no longer in a position to speak back to God a discovered explanation of reality. He could no longer dedicate to God's glory the results of his investigations and discoveries. He was not able, as the apostle was later to enjoin the Corinthian church, to "do all to the glory of God" (1 Cor. 10:31).

That, then, is the meaning of sin, the loss of ability and disposition to hold the honor and glory of God as paramount and determinative of action and behavior. A second result follows from our understanding of the state to which Adam's dereliction cast us. It is that because the competence to discharge the office of prophet had been evacuated, it was necessary that a Substitute should come to discharge that office in the place of sinners now shackled by defection. That points again to our conclusion as to the range of efficacy of the prophetic office of Christ.

Adam's sin consisted also in his inability to discharge his initially-mandated office as priest. What, then, is to be un-

---

[19] Adam's claim of *metaphysical autonomy* implied essentially the denial of his creaturehood and the assertion that as to his being he did not come from the hands of a Creator-God; that of *epistemological autonomy* implied that he was not dependent on God's revelation for the criteria of knowledge and understanding; and that of *ethical autonomy* implied that he could find within himself or within intramundane reality all necessary criteria of right behavior.

derstood as the essence of the office of priesthood? It may appear on the surface of things that it is described by the fact of sacrifice and the propitiation of God and his wrath against sin that has been so prominent in the Old Testament history of God's people. That may be due, no doubt, to the extensive history of the Levitical priesthood that God established as part of the Mosaic administration and to the respects in which the letter to the Hebrews sets the antitypical priesthood of Christ against the types of the sacrificial system of the Old Testament. The concept of sacrifice is, of course, essential to the meaning of the priestly office. But that office has a wider connotation and expression in fact.

Essential to the office of priesthood is the act of representation that the priest performed. Reflection on the Old Testament history discloses that representation was essential to the offices of both the prophet and the priest. The prophet represented God to the people, and the priest represented the people to God.[20] But by reason of that aspect of those offices, a significant characteristic was common to both. That was that the prophet and the priest were privileged to have direct communication with God (Deut. 18:15f; Num. 12:7-8). A relation with God that establishes the privilege of direct communication is, in the case we are now considering, of the essence of the priesthood.

That was the privilege that Adam enjoyed when the Second Person of the Godhead walked with him and spoke to him in the garden (Gen. 3:8). In the context in which Adam found himself by his creation, moreover, he was to discharge the office of priest by dedicating back to the glory of God all that he knew and found and discovered about the reality in which he was placed. And in that direct communication he was to worship his Creator-God. In short, the acts and facts of communication with God and the dedication of the human

---

[20] Compare the insightful discussion in Edward J. Young, *My Servants the Prophets* (Grand Rapids: Eerdmans, 1952), 102 and passim.

condition back to him, together with those of sacrifice and propitiation in the condition of fallenness that now exists, constitute the essence of the priesthood.

Again, however, by virtue of his fall into sin and of the disabilities that ensued, Adam was no longer able to discharge the office of priest to which he had been appointed. His sin again consisted in the fact that he had turned away from the mandated obligation to dedicate all aspects of his life, behavior, and experience to the glory of his Creator-God. A similar conclusion applies to the outcome of Adam's appointment to the office of king. He had been mandated to rule over all things to the glory of God. But again, that prerogative of derivative dominion had been abdicated. From that point on, the question remained as to the extent to which the common grace of God was to become effective in permitting Adam's offspring to exercise a degree of rule and authority over created reality. But to capsule his sorry state in a sentence, Adam in his postlapsarian state was disabled from discharging his appointed offices of prophet, priest, and king.

At this point we can draw together the threads of our argument and note its conclusion as to the scripturalness of the doctrine of the covenant of works. If, to recall our initial claim, God established with our first parents a covenant of works, what, we have asked, are the "works" of the covenant that thereby come into view? The answer lies on a twofold level. In the first place, the question is addressed to the condition of Adam in his pristine and prelapsarian state of holiness. At their most basic level, the works of the covenant were such that he should continue in that state and honor God in obedience to all of his mandated responsibilities and obligations. In that initial state he knew with an uncluttered naturalness what God required of him.[21] He knew what

---

[21] Adam's initial knowledge state, consistent with his creation in the image of God, is discussed further in Vickers, *Christian Confession*, chap. 3.

conformity to God's requirements of righteousness demanded. And of course, in his prelapsarian state he naturally loved God and walked in natural companionship with him. But the entrance of sin changed that. Secondly, the works of the covenant included preeminently, as has now been seen at adequate length, Adam's faithful discharge of the offices of prophet, priest, and king.

Against the obligations inherent in the covenant of works considered from the manward side, it is important to recognize also the Godward aspect of the relations inherent in that covenant. The terms of the covenant of works included the undertaking on God's part that on the grounds of his faithful works Adam would be rewarded with confirmation in holy character and entrance to eternal life. We are in no sense speaking here of "salvation by works." We are at this point speaking of our first parents' potential entitlement as that was suspended on a continuation in the state of original holiness in which they had been established. It would be a misconception of the highest order to confuse what is now being argued with the condition of salvation from sin. For considerations of salvation and redemption attain legitimacy and relevance only in the context of man's postlapsarian condition. In the context of our argument to this point, in the context of the absence of sin, the terms of the covenant of works have reference to the possibilities of the continuation of an unfallen state.

That issue informs in large part the objections raised in the next chapter against the dissent from the covenant of works. For it will be argued there that a confusion has entered the critical literature by reason of its conflation of the pre-Fall and the post-Fall situations as to the divine-human relation. The difference that exists between those two situations will be clarified further. But it can be stated in summary terms that in the whole of human history there have been only three persons who, by their works of obedience, could have merited God's favor and eternal and everlasting life. Two of those, our first parents while still in their state of innocence and freedom from sin, could have done so, but did not. The third, our substitute Redeemer, did. By his merit he earned eternal life for his people. That is the glory of the gospel of grace.

As to the Godward aspect of the relations inherent in the covenant of works, in that initial covenant God graciously bound himself to reward our first parents' works of faithful obedience. If our first parents had been faithful in discharging the responsibilities that their Creator had imposed upon them, then in accordance with God's sworn promise they would have merited, and would have been rewarded with, entrance into a state of eternal life. They would thereby have been confirmed in an eternal state of moral righteousness. That, in the shortest terms in which it can be put, is what we have referred to as a "works principle" coming to effect. That, to recall our earlier statement of it, is the conclusion that sits uneasily on unpracticed ears. It states in a sentence the remarkable fact that God did, in his covenantal promise to his creatures, place himself under an obligation to reward their faithfulness and obedience. That is the extent of the grace of God in creation.

Covenantal obligations

Our first parents did not sustain their probation and discharge to the glory of their Creator the obligations to which they were committed under the covenant of works. Their false assertion of autonomy shattered the pristine divine-human relation. But immediately following their Fall the promise of a redeemer was given (Gen. 3:15). God would in due time send his Son into the world as the substitute for his people, to discharge on their behalf the unfulfilled offices of prophet, priest, and king. He came into the world as Jesus Christ, and his identity as autotheotic, as fully God, Athanasius defended so effectively against the early Arian heresy. He would pay the penalty for the sins of his people in the sacrifice of satisfaction of which Anselm had spoken. But in what respect, it is necessary to ask, and to what extent have the obligations of the covenant of works continued and have relevance to the contemporary human condition?

It is not sufficient or appropriate to claim that "Man's sin destroyed the creation covenant and fractured his relationship with the Creator,"[22] or that "Adam's disobedience ... ended the covenant of creation."[23] For it remains to ask whether, rather than "destroying" or "ending" the covenant obligations, the works principle is of continuing relevance and normative significance. We answer in the affirmative on several grounds. In doing so we concur with the statement of the Westminster Confession that "God gave to Adam a law, as a *covenant of works*, by which he bound him, *and all his posterity* to personal, entire, exact, and perpetual obedience."[24] First, on the very grounds that the eternal justice and holiness of God are inviolable, it will be seen in the day of the consummation of all things that those who go to eternal perdition will do so on the grounds that their obligations under the covenant of works remain unfulfilled. To them it will be announced that "like Adam they have transgressed the covenant" (Hos. 6:7).

Second, "do this and ye shall live" (Lev. 18:5) remains the condition of life, clarified as it is in the statement of the apostle to the Romans that "the doers of the law will be justified" (Rom. 2:13). A. A. Hodge has commented that "This Covenant having been broken by Adam ... and Christ having fulfilled all of its conditions in behalf of all his people

---

[22] Robert P. Vande Kapelle and John D. Currid, "The Old Testament: The Covenant Between God and Man" in W. Andrew Hoffecker, ed., *Building a Christian World View* (Phillipsburg: P&R, 1986), 25.

[23] G. K. Beale and James Bibza, "The New Testament: The Covenant of Redemption in Jesus Christ," ibid., 49.

[24] Westminster Confession of Faith, XIX,I, italics added. The same insistence on the continuing normativity of the covenant of works is contained in Fisher's *Marrow of Modern Divinity*, 39, and more recently in Reymond, *New Systematic Theology*, 439.

... the covenant of works having been fulfilled by the second Adam is henceforth abrogated under the gospel. Nevertheless, since it is founded upon the principles of immutable justice, it still binds all men who have not fled to the refuge offered in the righteousness of Christ."[25]

It is not being said that the covenant of works remains as a way of eternal life. But third, while the covenant of works does not now continue as a way of entrance to life as it did in Adam's initial state, the sinner in his natural state remains exposed to the curse that the covenant contemplated. The original condition of life must be fulfilled. The justice and holiness of God demand nothing less. But as Hodge has just put it, for those who believe, rescue from the entailment of the failure to fulfill that condition resides in the fact that it has been fully met in the substitutionary work of Christ. Thus God has directed his soteric grace to meet the demands of his justice for the people he gave to his Son to redeem (John 17:6). That is the essence of what Anselm had stated in his doctrine of the atonement.

The covenant of works remains normative in the respect that it continues to place upon man the responsibility for perfect obedience to the obligations announced in the law of God. That is so, notwithstanding the fact that by reason of the inheritance of Adam's sinful state the power to live according to God's law has been lost. In other words, it has to be said that for the sinner, his responsibility is not suspended on his ability. Men are still "culpable before God and subject to death on the basis of the original covenant of works,"[26] because outside of Christ, upon whom God the Father laid the same obligation of perfect obedience that Adam had sustained, the obligation remains. Outside of Christ, there is no ground of approval by God. It has to be seen that the covenant of grace satisfies the redemptive requirements because it is a

---

[25] A. A. Hodge, *Outlines of Theology*, 314.
[26] Reymond, *New Systematic Theology*, 439.

"covenantal overlay" upon the covenant of works. By that it is meant that for the people he redeemed, the work of Christ under the terms of the covenant of grace has covered all of the unfulfilled requirements of the earlier covenant. Christ, the Second Adam, has met all the preceptive and penal demands of the covenant of works. He is in every respect the Substitute for his people. That is the glory of the gospel.

The biblical doctrine of the covenant of works, we observed at the beginning, has fallen on hard times. A strong and expanding dissent from the admissibility of the doctrine has emerged and will be addressed in the next chapter. If that dissent were allowed to stand, no lesser damage would be inflicted on Reformed doctrine than the effective dismissal of covenant theology. That would amount to what Kline has called "a radical renunciation of the Reformation."[27]

The elucidation of the doctrines of God's covenantal relations with man are essential to understanding the theological achievement of the Reformation. Contrary to the dissent we shall address in the next chapter, Reformation theology is covenantal theology. A recognition of the terms, the conditions, and the promises implicit in the covenant of works stands beside that of the covenant of grace for a full-orbed understanding of God's inscripturated revelation. The Reformation achievement lay in the rediscovery of the biblical doctrine of the work of Christ in satisfying the obligations that accrued to God's people by reason of their dereliction and their participation in the Adamic condition. In the fullest sense, Christ was the substitute for his people in fulfilling the demands of his office as prophet, priest, and king. The revelation of Christ, in his divine personhood and his obedience and total messianic accomplishment in this world, stands as the key to the Scriptures. For Christ came, and continues to be in his heavenly High Priestly session, the Lord of the Covenant.

---

[27] Kline, "Covenant Theology under Attack," 5.

Chapter 3

The Dissent from the Covenant of Works

The understanding of theological doctrine implicit in the preceding chapters is determined by the fundamental hermeneutical principle in terms of which we hear the Scriptures speak. That principle, Reformed theology recognizes, states that all of God's dealings with men and his disclosures to them have been, and are, covenantal. Reformed theology is covenantal theology. That refers to what has become known as "federal theology," which Peter A. Lillback describes as a system of theology in which "every detail is held together by the covenant, which is expressed in terms of a prelapsarian covenant with the first Adam and a postlapsarian covenant with the second Adam, namely, Jesus Christ."[1]

The genius of Reformed theology is that it has seen in the

---

[1] Peter A. Lillback, *The Binding of God: Calvin's Role in the Development of Covenant Theology* (Grand Rapids: Baker Academic, 2001), 27. See Lillback's discussion in op. cit. 26 on "Conflicting Definitions of Covenant Theology." Compare the discussion in A. A. Hodge, *Outlines of Theology*, 362-66.

Scriptures the revelation of successive divinely established covenants. The covenant of redemption, designed in an eternal agreement between the Persons of the Godhead and involving the distribution of redemptive offices among them, determined the scope, the prospects, and the processes of the sinner's redemption from the entailment of sin. The covenant of grace, the parties to which were God on the one hand and his people as represented by Christ on the other, came to effect for the purpose of implementing the terms of the covenant of redemption. It was designed to bring to consummation the objectives that the covenant of redemption had set forth.[2] The objectives of redemption that were thus contemplated are referable, of course, to the fallen condition to which mankind had been reduced by Adam's sin. But precedent to the salvific process that was thereby instituted, God graciously established a covenant of works with Adam in his initial, holy, and prelapsarian state. We have already inspected the terms, the conditions, and the promises of it.

It is precisely on that level that a contemporary dissent from all we have said of the covenant of works has been made. In the interest of theological orthodoxy it is necessary to look briefly at the terms in which the dissent from the

---

[2] See Witsius, *Economy of the Covenants*, 1:165, "Of the Covenant between God the Father and God the Son," and idem, 281, "Of the Covenant of God with the elect." Charles Hodge has written approvingly of Witsius' doctrinal formulation. See Hodge, *Systematic Theology*, 2:358ff. Hodge's doctrinal argument, which is worthy of close inspection, concludes with reference to "the covenant of redemption between the Father and the Son, and the covenant of grace between God and his people [that] the latter supposes the former and is founded upon it." A discussion of the historic Reformed doctrine of the covenants is contained in A. A. Hodge, *Evangelical Theology* (Edinburgh: Banner of Truth, 1976), 163ff. See also the critical summary and extensive historical review, bearing particularly on the covenant of works, in Rowland S. Ward, *God and Adam: Reformed Theology and the Creation Covenant* (Wantirna, Australia: New Melbourne Press, 2003).

covenant of works has been expressed. Spearheading that dissent has been the work of Daniel Fuller in his rejection of covenantal theology. He dissents bluntly from the long-established and orthodox claims of that Reformed system of doctrine. He recognizes, but forthrightly rejects, its claim that "when Jesus came to earth, he fulfilled the covenant of meritorious works that Adam and Eve broke."[3] Fuller's thesis negates what has to be seen as the meaning of the substitutionary work of Christ in its fullest aspects. The Reformed theological tradition has been seriously infected by the dissent to which we have referred. Support for that occurs in claims advanced by John Piper, who is well known for his many valuable contributions to the evangelical testimony. He has stated in his foreword to the work by his mentor, Fuller, that "No book besides the Bible has had a greater influence on my life than Daniel Fuller's *The Unity of the Bible*." Piper joins in Fuller's dismissal of covenant theology, stating that he understood God's law when it "stopped being at odds with the gospel [and] stopped being a job description for earning wages under a so-called covenant of works (which I never could find in the Bible)." Piper reflects Fuller's statement that "sin is essentially unbelief, contrary to Calvin and covenant theology, which declares that Adam and Eve's sin was a failure to render a full measure of the meritorious works God had spelled out in his 'job description.'"[4] Such a conclusion, which flies in the face of the historic Reformed doctrine of the covenants, misconstrues the meaning and essence of God's

---

[3] Daniel P. Fuller, *The Unity of the Bible* (Grand Rapids: Zondervan, 1992), 181. The current evangelical rejection of the covenant of works has been replied to effectively by Kline, "Covenant Theology under Attack."

[4] John Piper's foreword to *The Unity of the Bible*, page x, and Fuller, op. cit, 185. See also the reference below to a work by Scott J. Hafemann who acknowledges his indebtedness to his "formative professors, Drs. John Piper and Daniel Fuller," *The God of Promise and the Life of Faith* (Wheaton: Crossway Books, 2001), 13.

initial covenant with Adam. To state, with Piper, that the covenant of works involved a "job description for earning wages" diminishes beyond acceptance the honor of God in his having bound himself, as has already been seen, to reward Adam on the grounds of his covenantal obedience.

John Piper has recently presented a valuable exegetical study in refutation of Robert Gundry's rejection of the classic Reformed doctrine of imputation.[5] A brief comment on it will illustrate the present state of doctrinal exposition as it relates to our present discussion.

Piper has ably defended the biblical doctrine that the believer's justification rests in the imputation to him of the righteousness of Christ. But of crucial import is the ground on which that imputation has been made available in the wisdom and purposes of God. It rests, it needs to be said with equal clarity, on the fact that the guilt of the sinner's sin was imputed to Christ. In the redemptive purposes of God a reciprocal imputation has occurred. By the imputation of our guilt to Christ he was *constituted* guilty, in order that the Father could *declare* him guilty and impose upon him the penalty of our sin. Reciprocally, God has *constituted* the sinner righteous by imputing to him, thereby granting him the possession of, the righteousness of Christ, in order to be able to *declare* him righteous. More precisely, the imputation of *forensic guilt* to Christ, constituting him guilty (though not, of course, constituting him a sinner), and the imputation of *forensic righteousness* to the sinner, thereby constituting him righteous, is the reciprocal transaction precedent to the sinner's justification.

Piper has rightly spoken of "the imputation of our sin to Christ."[6] But there does not come to clear expression in his argument the meaning of that latter imputation in its total

---

[5] John Piper, *Counted Righteous in Christ: Should We Abandon the Imputation of Christ's Righteousness?* (Wheaton: Crossway Books, 2002).
[6] Op. cit., 69.

relevance to the sinner's guilt. The argument does not therefore proceed to the level that has occupied us in our present discussion, namely, the respect in which the sinner's guilt derived from his repudiation of obligations sustained under the covenant of works. For that reason the work of Christ is inadequately construed, in that it is not clearly displayed as accomplishing for us precisely what he came to do in fulfilling the previously unfulfilled obligations of the covenant of works. Piper has recognized that "by his obedience he [the Second Adam] fulfilled what Adam failed to do."[7] But he has not developed that insight adequately to clarify the all-important covenantal reference we have adduced. It is in that fuller covenantal respect that the substitutionary character of Christ's identity and work is to be understood. Piper has spoken of the fact that "sin creates a real guilt that makes a person feel despairing and hopeless."[8] But it needs to be understood that the primary meaning of guilt, as it is relevant to our present discussion, is not such personal awareness of despair and inadequacy. In shortest terms, guilt resides in the fact and the consciousness of unfulfilled obligations. It is that guilt to which the work of Christ is addressed and that was imputed to him. Piper's avoidance of the relevance of the work of Christ to the sinner's obligations under the covenant of works is related to his endorsement of Daniel Fuller's forthright rejection of that covenant.[9]

Adam, on the grounds of his obedience and therefore his satisfying what we have referred to as the "works principle," would have merited the reward to which God had covenantally committed himself. But it is that doctrinal conclusion

---

[7] Ibid., 103
[8] Ibid., 78.
[9] This seems relevant to what Piper acknowledges in his lengthy footnote on ibid, page 100, "I do not yet understand." The people between Adam and Moses, to whom Piper refers in that context, did in fact have a law and were responsible to it, namely, the law inherent in the covenant of works.

that some contemporary theologians are unwilling to acknowledge. That is instanced again by Scott J. Hafemann,[10] who concludes that "before Adam and Eve sinned they were *already* enjoying eternal life as made possible by God's magnificent gifts of grace; they were not trying to prove themselves during a probation period in order to gain the right to eat of the tree of life and thereby gain a higher state of holiness or spiritual existence."[11] Hafemann's conclusion that "there is no such thing as a *merited* promise in the Bible,"[12] conflates the status and responsibilities of prelapsarian and postlapsarian man. It fails to distinguish the terms of the covenant of works from those of God's soteric relation to sinners in their fallen state. Any apparent intention on Hafemann's part to soften the Fuller-Piper thesis by speaking of "The Covenant Structure of the Bible" fails by reason of his conclusion that again rejects the Reformed doctrine of the covenant of works. "The covenant relationship established in the Garden of Eden," Hafemann concludes, "provides the basis and contours of the relationship that exists between God and his people throughout history."[13] It follows that "the insight that there is *one uniform* covenant relationship that runs throughout the various covenants of the Bible means that we no longer divide the Bible into two conflicting messages ... a 'covenant of works' versus a 'covenant of grace.'"[14] In

---

[10] Scott J. Hafemann, *The God of Promise and the Life of Faith*.

[11] Ibid., 53. Hafemann's claim as to Adam's "already enjoying eternal life" may be read in the light of the comment by Geerhardus Vos, in his "The Doctrine of the Covenant in Reformed Theology," republished in Richard B. Gaffin, Jr., ed., *Redemptive History and Biblical Interpretation* (Phillipsburg: Presbyterian and Reformed, 1980), 234-267, that as to the doctrine of the covenant of works, "According to the Lutherans man had already reached his destination in that God had placed him in a state of uprightness. Eternal life was already in his possession," 242.

[12] Ibid., 58.

[13] Ibid., 55.

[14] Ibid., 59. Here Hafemann concurs with Fuller's claim of a "continuum" referred to below. That is made clear in the long footnote in

that conclusion, the Fuller-Piper thesis remains intact. There is no room for a covenant of works. The relationship between God and our first parents that the Reformed doctrine of the covenant of works has contemplated has not, we are told, ever existed.

At issue in our present discussion is the status of Adam as the beneficiary of God's gracious covenant and promises of benediction in response to works of obedience and malediction in the event of disobedience. The status and obligations of prelapsarian and postlapsarian man, and the distinguishable structures of the divine-human relation in the respective situations, should not be allowed to confuse the terms and outcomes of the covenant of works and the covenant of grace. Herman Witsius, the seventeenth-century theologian who gave us his important work on the covenants, *The Economy of the Covenants between God and Man*, clearly insisted on the distinction we have in view. Witsius states, "Nothing is here to be brought in which does not belong to the covenant of works, the promises of that covenant, and the duties of man under the same; all which are most distinct from the covenant of grace."[15] It is not being said that the terms and the redemptive objectives of the covenant of grace are unrelated to the outcome of Adam's probation under the covenant of works. Of course a relation of high importance exists. But in our present discussion we are saying with Witsius that all that is properly contemplatable as to the work of Christ that followed our first parents' dereliction "belongs to another covenant."[16] There should not be any conflation of the pre-Fall and the post-Fall divine-human relations and covenants as has been erroneously suggested.

Hafemann, *The God of Promise*, 226-228, where he explicitly rejects the doctrine that by virtue of Adam and Eve's dereliction in their "probationary period ... Christ keeps the Law or 'covenant of works' perfectly and then gives to us the blessing he has earned," idem. 227.
[15] Witsius, *Economy of the Covenants*, 1:106.
[16] Idem.

Daniel Fuller's forthright rejection of covenantal theology is a continuation of the argument he had presented earlier.[17] As Meredith Kline has observed in his "Covenant Theology under Attack," Fuller there "rejects [the contrast] between gospel grace and the works principle.... Fuller's refusal to acknowledge a works/grace contrast ... is part of his broader insistence that the divine-human relationship never entails a works principle.... He repudiates covenant theology not only in its recognition of a works principle in the Law, but in its identification of God's original covenant with Adam as a covenant of works." Kline there places the works principle firmly within the Scriptural articulation of God's prelapsarian covenant with Adam. In short, where covenant theology differentiates "the pre-Fall covenant and the subsequent covenant of grace" Fuller sees a "continuum" of grace. In dismissing the covenant of works, Fuller and his followers misunderstand the ground on which the gospel of grace stands. It stands on the fact that "Jesus ... merited it [grace] for us by his perfect fulfillment of the covenant of works."[18] Fuller can in that way counter-claim, "I will keep stressing that all obedience to God is an 'obedience that comes from faith,' and never an obedience of works."[19] Thus, as Fuller has constructed the prelapsarian relation, Adam's dereliction was not in essence a failure of works of obedience, but a failure of faith.[20]

---

[17] Daniel P. Fuller, *Gospel and Law: Contrast or Continuum?* (Grand Rapids: Eerdmans, 1980).

[18] See Fuller, *The Unity of the Bible*, 181.

[19] Idem, 182.

[20] See the review of Fuller's *Gospel and Law: Contrast or Continuum*, by O. Palmer Robertson, in *Presbyterion*, VIII, 1, Spring 1982, and Fuller's rejoinder in "A Response on the Subjects of Works and Grace," *Presbyterion*, 1983. See also in the same issue of *Presbyterion*, W. Robert Godfrey, "Back to Basics: A Response to the Robertson-Fuller Dialogue," and Meredith G. Kline, "Of Works and Grace."

The grounds of dissent from the covenant of works

The grounds on which the dissent from the covenant of works has been made are primarily fourfold. First, to bring into focus the point of principal concern, the claim is rejected that God covenantally bound himself to reward our first parents on the grounds of their meritorious works of obedience. The claim is rejected that God's rewarding Adam on the grounds of his meritorious obedience would have been simply consonant with God's justice, grounded as that was in the conditional promise of blessing that God had given. There could not have been, the dissenting thesis claims, any grounds of human merit, in any respect or at any point of the Creator-creature relation. All such relations must be grounded simply in the unmerited grace of God. Further, the defect in Adam's dereliction, it is claimed, was not primarily and principally in his failure on the level of works, but in his failure of belief and faith.

The wish to advance and preserve the honor of the grace of God, prominent as that is in the literature of dissent from the covenant of works, is, of course, commendable at all relevant points of doctrinal theology. But the dissent we now have in view fails by reason of several damaging misconceptions. Of principal significance, it overlooks entirely the fact that the Second Adam, in the human nature he took into union with his divine nature, provided the very meritorious work to which Adam was obligated but failed to perform.

Further, the dissent on this principal ground fails to see that it was the Father's rewarding the meritorious obedience of the Second Adam that warrants the conclusion that a corresponding prospect of reward was available to the first Adam, for the first was a type of the second. Adam was "the figure of him that was to come" (Rom. 5:14).[21]

---

[21] That conclusion has been succinctly stated by Thornwell, "Whatever, therefore, Christ has purchased, Adam might have gained," *The*

It is also argued in this connection that the infinitely holy and eternal God could not have bound himself in covenant to reward the meritorious works of his initially-established creature, and that all aspects of the divine-human relation should be interpreted in terms of the unmerited grace of God. But in that argument the meaning of God's grace is diminished and not clearly understood. For God's covenantal binding of himself is, in itself, a culminating act of the grace of creation. In other words, it is an inadequate doctrine of the grace of God that confines it to its obvious and clear soteric dimension. That it is by the grace of God that the sinner is saved is beyond argument (Eph. 2:8). The very heart of the gospel is evacuated if that reality is denied. But in the grace of God as displayed in the terms of the covenant of works no such salvific intention is, or could have been, in view. Rather, the condescending grace of God is at that point referable to the prospect of confirming our first and unfallen parents in their holy character.

The important matter of the meaning of the grace of God, as that has reference to his pristine relations with man, has been subject to varying interpretations in the Reformed literature. Many authors have confined the meaning of grace to "God's blessing of man in spite of his demerits [and therefore] we ought not apply the term grace to the pre-Fall situation."[22] Our conclusion, however, implied in what has been said, is that God's establishing a covenant of works with Adam was itself an act of his condescension and *grace*, but that his rewarding Adam for his obedience would have been an act of his *justice*. That, it can be suggested, puts the Law-Gospel debate in appropriate perspective.

Our statement that God established the covenant of works as an act of grace is consistent with that taken by a number of

---

Collected Writings of James Henley Thornwell (Edinburgh: Banner of Truth, 4 vols., 1974), 1:288.
[22] Kline, "Covenant Theology under Attack," www as cited, 2.

authors in the Reformed tradition. To adduce three prominent nineteenth-century American theologians, Shedd states that "God *graciously* entered into a covenant with holy Adam."[23] Dabney concludes that "God's act of entering into a covenant with Adam [was] one of pure *grace* and condescension.... God, therefore, moved by pure *grace*, condescended to establish a covenant with his holy creature, in virtue of which a temporary obedience might be *graciously* accepted as a ground for God's communicating Himself to him, and assuring him ever after of holiness, happiness, and communion with God."[24] Thornwell similarly observed, "This dispensation [God's initial relation with, and revelation to, Adam] is known as a Covenant of Works,"[25] and he preceded that definition by exclaiming, "Surely, our God is *grace*; the first covenant proves it as truly as the second!"[26]

Certainly the grace of God in its subsequent address to our fallen condition is adequately interpretable only in terms of its salvific intention. And certainly, the justice of God required and demanded that the obligations of the covenant of works should be honored in human nature; the honor of God's justice would have been violated if that had not, in the final issue, been satisfied. It was precisely the preservation of that honor that was accomplished by the Second Adam in his substitutionary redemptive obedience. The dissent from the covenant of works, by insisting that any eternal benefit with which Adam might have been blessed should be attributable to the grace, and not the justice, of God misunderstands and misplaces the meaning and import of grace.

That is so, notwithstanding suggestions in earlier literature that Adam's potential reward was suspended, not merito-

---

[23] Shedd, *Dogmatic Theology*, 2:152, italics added.
[24] Dabney, *Lectures in Systematic Theology* (Grand Rapids: Zondervan, 1972), 302, italics added.
[25] Thornwell, *Collected Writings*, 1:268.
[26] Idem, 1:266, italics added.

riously on his work of obedience, but simply on the grace of God. Arguments to that effect occurred at several points in the history of Reformed theology. Murray, as anticipated earlier, comments, "The term [covenant of works] is not felicitous, for the reason that the elements of grace entering into the administration are not properly provided by the term 'works'.... From the promise of the Adamic administration we must dissociate all notions of meritorious reward."[27] The Westminster Confession appears ambivalent on the point, referring in VII, II to a "covenant of works" but in VII, I simply to "some voluntary condescension on God's part." The Westminster Shorter Catechism refers in its Question 12 to a "covenant of life." Turretin comments, "By his own right, God could indeed have prescribed obedience to man (created by him) without any promise of reward. But in order to temper that supreme dominion with goodness, he added a covenant consisting in the promise of reward and the stipulation of obedience." Turretin then continues, "Since man has all things from and owes all to God, he can seek from him nothing as his own by right, nor can God be a debtor to him – not by condignity of work ... because that can bear no proportion to the infinite reward of life."[28] John Owen states that "the promises ... did in strict justice exceed the worth of the obedience required, and so was a superadded effect of goodness and grace."[29] Sinclair Ferguson interprets Owen as saying that "even if a man were to keep the covenant of works, he would acquire no merit."[30] Thomas Boston states, "Man was ... at God's disposal.... There was no proportion

---

[27] Murray, *Collected Writings*, 2:49, 56. Karlberg suggests, "The position of John Murray is in many ways analogous to that of Fuller," "Reformed Interpretation of the Mosaic Covenant," 38, n.97 and 48-53.
[28] Turretin, *Elenctic Theology,* 574-78.
[29] John Owen, *An Exposition of the Epistle to the Hebrews* (Grand Rapids: Baker, 7 vols., 1980), 2:337.
[30] Ferguson, *John Owen on the Christian Life* (Edinburgh: Banner of Truth, 1987), 23.

between the work and the promised reward."³¹ Geerhardus Vos, who has provided a valuable history of the doctrine of the covenant of works and the covenant of grace, concludes, with reference to the prelapsarian covenant: "Good works in the first covenant were not strictly meritorious, but were richly rewarded by free favor."³²

The second level on which the dissent from the covenant of works has been entered is the claim that Adam's dereliction was a failure not of required works of obedience, but of belief and faith.³³ But that again fails by reason that it misunderstands the meaning of both faith and works, by setting them in a false and unsustainable opposition. We are not concerned at this stage to enter the discussion of the place of works as they might or might not confer salvific competence on the sinner. We have already insisted that salvation is by grace through faith, and not by works. Nor are we concerned to address the question of the relation between faith and works in the ongoing life of the Christian believer, or the prospect of the believer's eternal reward as that is suspended on the grace of good works in this life. The question confronting us at this point is that of the relation in the initial Adamic condition between his belief, trust, and commitment to God his Creator on the one hand, and his works of obedience on the other. In his works of obedience belief and faith would come to their fullest expression. There was then a harmony, a projection of faith to works of obedience, not an opposition, between them.

Thirdly, the dissent from the covenant of works states that Adam could not have merited reward on the grounds of his works of obedience because a discrepancy or a dispropor-

---

[31] Boston, *Human Nature in its Fourfold State* (Edinburgh: Banner of Truth, 1964), 49.

[32] Vos, "The Doctrine of the Covenant in Reformed Theology," 240.

[33] Here Fuller's misleading "continuum" thesis as referred to above again becomes relevant. Fuller mistakenly sees "the obedience of faith" as exclusively operative in the matter of man's warranting God's blessing in all stages and at all times in the divine-human relation.

tion would necessarily exist between the infinitely valuable reward of eternal confirmation in a holy state and the lesser value of Adam's finite obedience. But it can be rejoined in that connection that Adam's work of obedience would bring pleasure and satisfaction to God that would confer an infinite value on the works themselves.[34] The potential value of Adam's works of obedience can be set against the infinite outrage of God's holiness that Adam's sin occasioned and the infinite and eternal punishment it deserved. When the dissent claims that Adam's reward could not have accrued on the grounds of such a meritorious obedience, and that it must therefore be ascribable to the unmerited grace of God rather than to his covenantal justice, that dissent is again misconstruing both God's justice and his grace. Moreover, if such a notion of disproportionality were held to argue against God's rewarding a finite merit with infinitely-valued reward, it would have to be concluded logically that a finite demerit could not properly be rewarded with infinite wrath and eternal perdition. If that were so, the very promise of malediction contained in God's initial covenant (Gen. 2:17) would have to be vacated as itself unjust. That is the dilemma into which the dissenting argument collapses.

The fourth ground of dissent from the covenant of works returns us to Daniel Fuller's basic thesis. The failure of the dissent at that point is of major proportions, attacking the heart of the gospel of redemption. For not only is it true, from the interpretative perspectives of classic Reformed theology, that if Christ did not complete on our behalf the requirements of the covenant of works we would be left without a title to heaven. That can be put in another way. If, as the dissenting thesis maintains, there was no works principle in terms of which Adam could have merited reward, then there must also

---

[34] This point has been made in Kline, "Covenant Theology under Attack," www as cited, 3, and in Reymond, *New Systematic Theology*, 433.

have been no satisfaction of an unfulfilled works principle by Christ. If, again, the first Adam's entry to eternal life would have been only by grace and not by works, then a corresponding conclusion would follow with respect to the Second Adam, of whom the first was typical. Christ would then have been rewarded, not for his work of obedience, but again simply as an act of God the Father's grace. The further and alarming result follows from the dissenting thesis, then, that the rejection of the works principle that is inherent in that initial covenant, and that came to its full expression in the substitutionary obedience of Christ, leaves the dissenters to introduce indirectly into their so-called gospel of salvation another level of works. That is the case because if the merit of the work of Christ is not available for imputation to those who believe in him, then the believer is left to satisfy the inexorable justice of God on his own behalf. Then in spite of claims to the contrary, the contemplated good works of sanctification are collapsed into works amenable to justification. That misconception emerges explicitly in Fuller's claim that in many passages in Scripture "good works are made the instrumental cause of justification."[35] That implicit confusion of the scope and meaning and processes of justification and sanctification, implicit, it now appears, in Fuller's oft-stated but ambiguous "obedience of faith," finally evacuates the dissenting thesis of any possibility of validity and meaning.

It is noteworthy that in his review of Daniel Fuller's *Gospel and Law*, Robertson comments on Fuller's confusion between justification and sanctification in the latter's understanding of Paul's objectives in the Galatian letter.[36] Kline observes even more pointedly that because the Fuller school fails to accord proper significance to the work of Christ in his active obedience, "the resultant tendency is to confuse

---

[35] Fuller, "A Response on the Subjects of Works and Grace," *Presbyterion*, 1983, 79.
[36] Robertson, *Presbyterion*, VIII, 1, Spring 1982.

justification and sanctification in a new legalism in which the role of good works, which was not permitted to enter through the front door [by the substitutionary work of Christ as construed in its satisfying previously unfulfilled obligations of the covenant of works], now sneaks in the back door. What Christ could not do is left for us to do, somehow."[37]

Note should be taken of Fuller's conclusion that *"the condition for justification is persevering faith."*[38] That conclusion suggests an alignment with recent discussions that have diminished the doctrine of forensic justification. The latter turns on the declarative statement of God based on the reciprocal imputation of the sinner's sin to Christ and Christ's righteousness to the sinner. That diminution of doctrine is exhibited in Norman Shepherd's *The Call of Grace: How the Covenant Illuminates Salvation and Evangelism*, where it is argued that the obedience of "good works," notably the works of the Christian believer within the orbit of his Christian life, is not to be understood as "the evidence of salvation," but as "the essence of salvation."[39] Fuller's argument is not rescued from the confusion it has sown by his statement that "a person's sins are forgiven the moment he or she believes."[40] To suggest that Fuller's argument regarding perseverance intends to save covenantal theology from a lapse into antinomianism would fail to see the far-reaching damage his work has inflicted on the doctrine of the covenant of works.

Christ, substitute prophet, priest, and king

The recent dissent from the covenant of works should not deflect from the earlier conclusion that by reason of our first

---

[37] Kline, "Covenant Theology under Attack," www as cited, 4.
[38] Fuller, *The Unity of the Bible*, 310.
[39] Shepherd, op. cit., 104. See the discussion in Vickers, *Christian Confession*, 150-51.
[40] Fuller, *The Unity of the Bible*, 318.

parents' failure to merit the reward that had been conditionally promised to them they were disabled from discharging their offices of prophet, priest, and king. It was necessary that Christ should come as the substitute to discharge those offices on the sinner's behalf. A less than robust understanding of the covenant of works and its unfulfilled obligations diminishes the redemptive work of Christ in those respects. The redemptive work of Christ will be discussed more fully at a later stage, after a further exploration has been made of the state of the soul in sin and its implications for the human condition. But we can anticipate briefly at this stage some respects in which Christ discharged those substitutionary offices.

In the light of the reciprocal promises of blessing and curse contained in the covenantal relation that God established with Adam, it was not possible that Adam could reestablish his pristine relation with God by a renewed obedience. He could not by his own decision and action obliterate the state of sin and misery to which he had fallen. The entailment of sin that descended on him, and the bequest that descended on all who followed him by ordinary generation, meant that redemption by his or their own works was not possible. For God and man were now at enmity. "The carnal mind is enmity against God" (Rom. 8:7). Man is now a God-hater (Rom. 1:30). An enmity has replaced the pristine friendship between God and man and could henceforth be removed only by God's redemptive grace and his initiative in establishing peace by the work of his Son (Rom. 5:1). Some brief answers to the question of our Lord's work of substitution will disclose the essential principles that are involved.

First, when we were unable to glorify God by discharging the office of prophet, or the office and task of understanding and explaining the meaning of the created reality, Christ came to discharge that office for us. He did that by showing us that "in [him] are hid all the treasures of wisdom and knowledge" (Col. 2:3), and that it is he "by [whom] all things consist" or are upheld (Col. 1:17). He has given us thereby the principles and categories of explanation of all things. He has shown us that nothing in this world is properly understandable unless it is seen as constituted by the facts that he thought before the foundation of the world, and which he has ordered by his providence in the historical time he created as the mode of our existence. In our condition of derivative, human finitude we understand anything only as we understand it as belonging to Christ, and as an aspect of the universe of reality that is constituted by facts that he established and that operate according to his created laws. He alone provides us with the principles of interpretation that give us an entry to true knowledge and understanding.

Because in this way Christ provides us with the principles of interpretation and understanding, all of the facts and all of the constellations of facts that we encounter in our search for knowledge must be Christologically interpreted. In addition to Christ's office and function in those respects as our substitute prophet, he is our prophet in that he "reveals to us the will of God for our salvation,"[41] and by his Spirit he sensitizes us to the meaning of the holy law of God by which we are called to live.

Second, Christ is our substitute priest. When, as a result of Adam's fall, we forfeited the priestly privilege of direct communion with God, Christ came in order to be our mediator with the Father. As the apostle put it, "Through him [Christ] we both have access by one Spirit unto the Father" (Eph. 2:18). The glory of Christ, who is himself God in human nature, exists in the fact that now, in the heavens and for ever, he lives at the right hand of God the Father to represent us and to make continual intercession for us. And "when he appears we shall be like him" (1 John 3:2), sinless at last, established in his image, and reestablished into the perfection of our essential personhood, in the holiness of human nature that our Lord assumed as the Second Adam.

[41] Westminster Shorter Catechism, Question 24.

The efficacy of Christ's faithful discharge of his priestly office, in which he himself became the offering for sin and the priest who administered the offering, was such that in recognition of his achievement he was raised to the position of authority and rule at the right hand of the Father (Heb. 1:3). That very fact expands its significance to convey to the Christian all of his eschatological hope and prospects.

Third, Christ came into the world to discharge for us the office of king, the performance of which we had vacated by Adam's fall. The possibility of our dominion over created reality in fulfillment of Adam's creation mandate (Gen. 1:28) has been rehabilitated to an extent by the operation of God's common grace. But our fuller inheritance and privilege of dominion has been reestablished by Christ and our union with him. Its full realization awaits the culmination of our eternal reign with him. It is clear on the surface of the Scriptures that Christ came to establish a kingdom in which we shall reign jointly with him. He has "made us unto our God kings and priests; and we shall reign with him on the earth" (Rev. 5:10).

Conclusion

We conclude with a twofold observation. First, God's covenantal dealings with us came to expression initially in the covenant of creation, referred to as the covenant of works. That established the obligations to our Creator-God which, in Adam's fall, we repudiated, but which God had placed himself under obligation to reward had Adam sustained his probation. Second, those obligations were assumed by our substitute and Redeemer, the Second Adam, the Second Person of the Godhead. He came into this world as Jesus Christ in order to reveal God the Father to us, to satisfy the demands of God's covenantal law for us, and to reconcile us to God. Further, and in order to accomplish the redemptive objectives to which he had committed himself, Christ identified himself with us in all of the actions in this world that were addressed to that end.

The covenant of works continues with normative significance and projects its demands with eternally relevant import. But the glory of the gospel is that God is now at peace with his people (Rom. 5:1), and "there is therefore now no condemnation to them which are in Christ Jesus" (Rom. 8:1).

Addendum: The question of merit and the prelapsarian covenant

We have observed in the foregoing that in the history of Reformed theology a divergence of view has existed as to the place, if any, of merit in relation to the prelapsarian covenant, the covenant of works. The statements attributed there to Murray, Turretin, Owen, and Ferguson are to be read in the light of a long discussion on the point. Shedd takes note of the opinion of Witsius that we have adduced, to the effect that "God by his promise, has made himself a debtor to men," and he notes a similar statement by Augustine that "God became our debtor ... by promising what he pleased."[42] Dabney, to the contrary, concluded, "In the strict sense, then, no work of man brings God in the doer's debt, to reward him.... No work of man to God can bring Him, by its own intrinsic merit, under obligation to reward."[43] In the same vein, A. A. Hodge concludes, "Under the covenant of works, God graciously promised to reward the obedience of Adam with eternal life. That was a reward, however, not of merit, but of free grace."[44] But Charles Hodge, to the contrary again, observed, "Had [Adam] retained his integrity he would have *merited* the promised blessing."[45]

It will have been noted from the foregoing also that a difference of view as to the scope and terms of the prelapsarian

---

[42] Shedd, *Dogmatic Theology*, 1:368.
[43] Dabney, *Lectures in Systematic Theology*, 680.
[44] Hodge, *Outlines of Theology*, 528.
[45] Hodge, *Systematic Theology*, 2:364, italics added.

relation between God and Adam has arisen within the community of scholars who hold a commitment to the essentials of federal theology. Some are sympathetic with Murray's disinclination to retain the classic designation of a covenant of works and his holding to the primacy of grace. Others, with Kline for example, are more ready to find within the Scriptural data not only a covenant of works but also a potential merit in what might have been Adam's obedience. The debate that has ensued has been discussed effectively by Jeong Koo Jeon,[46] and Tim J. R. Trumper has published an insightful review of that work.[47]

These divergences of view reflect differences that arose at the time of the Reformation, as Lillback has made clear.[48] In his chapter, "Is There a Covenant of Works in Calvin's Theology?,"[49] Lillback takes note of arguments pro and con and reaches an affirmative answer to the question. He notes "Calvin's acceptance of a pre-fall covenant ... *although denying any merit to Adam's obedience*,"[50] and adds, "If the covenant of works required merit... this could never be applied to Calvin's prelapsarian covenant."[51]

As to merit, we have argued in the preceding text that Christ, the Second Adam, performed the meritorious work required under the covenant of works that the first Adam had failed to sustain. As a result, by God's gracious act of substitution the merit that Christ obtained is imputed to his people. They were themselves in dereliction by reason of Adam's fall.

---

[46] Jeong Koo Jeon, *Covenant Theology: John Murray's and Meredith Kline's response to the Historical Development of Federal Theology in Reformed Thought* (Langham, Md.: University Press of America, 1999).

[47] T. J. R. Trumper, *Westminster Theological Journal*, Fall 2002, 387-404.

[48] Peter A. Lillback, *The Binding of God*, passim.

[49] Ibid., 276ff.

[50] Ibid., 304, italics added.

[51] Ibid., 300.

It is useful, then, in considering the conclusion that Lillback has attributed to Calvin, to look more closely at what we are to understand as his position. The question at issue is twofold: first, whether we are to understand that God "bound himself to promises of potential benediction and malediction" and thereby obligated himself to reward Adam's potential meritorious obedience; and second, whether we may legitimately conclude, as a result, that God's rewarding Adam should be considered to have been a response to earned merit on Adam's part, or as purely a response of grace on God's part. What is at issue, in other words, is whether Adam's potential reward would have been grounded in God's grace or in his justice.

Lillback's treatise addresses the question of "The Covenant of Law and the Question of Merit and Grace before Adam's Fall." His conclusion is consistent with his claim that "Calvin develops the prelapsarian experience of Adam in language consonant with the covenant of works"[52] and with his summary: "This discussion of the prelapsarian covenant and its sacrament dates from the first edition of the *Institutes* published in 1536. Calvin's theological writing began with a notion of a pre-fall covenant!"[53] It is acknowledged that "Calvin's rudimentary or inchoative covenant of works is, to be sure, incompletely defined or developed. Its existence however, seems in certain ways to adumbrate the covenant of works of the federalists."[54]

But while it may be concluded that Calvin held to a prelapsarian covenant, or, in other words, to a covenant of works in the sense that has been indicated, the question remains as to whether he conceived of the presence of potential merit in that covenant, in the manner in which we have construed it. To answer that question it should be noted, first, that in his commentary on Ezekiel. 20:11 Calvin observes that "God

---

[52] Ibid., 289, cf. 289-91.
[53] Ibid., 291.
[54] Idem.

graciously *binds himself* to us by this promise,"[55] and it is on the grounds of that "gracious binding" of himself that God holds forth the prospect of reward for obedience. Calvin having said in commenting on Genesis 15:6 that "works are not meritorious, *except under the covenant of the law*,"[56] affirmed merit by the covenant of law. He thereby sees, as Lillback puts it, "the covenant of law that provided for salvation by merit was still gracious."[57] But it is to be noted that it was this Calvinian claim of the promise of life by merit for obedience under the covenant of law (in the Mosaic administration) that was taken over by the federal theology to explain the same matter in the covenant of works.

It should be observed, however, that when Calvin refers here to the covenant of law he has in view the Mosaic administration of the covenant of grace. It still appears, therefore, that he did not employ what we have just seen as his "gracious-merit" concept to the law in a prelapsarian context.[58] That was because central to Calvin's thought was the fact, as he saw it, that no creature of God, even if he obeyed God perfectly and had done all that was required of him, could merit anything from God. Calvin comments on Romans 11:35 that "Paul not only concludes, that God owes us nothing, on account of our corrupt and sinful nature; but he denies, that *if man were perfect*, he could bring anything before God, by which he could gain his favour."[59] The question of merit in the pre-fall covenant therefore remains open at this stage. It remained for the later proponents of federal theology, to some of whom we have referred, to make the move that explicitly

---

[55] Calvin, comm. loc. cit., trans. Thomas Myers, *Calvin's Commentaries* (Grand Rapids: Baker, vol. XII, 1979), 297-98, italics added.
[56] Calvin, comm. loc. cit., trans. John King, *Calvin's Commentaries* (Grand Rapids; Baker, vol. I, 1979), 409, italics added.
[57] Lillback, *The Binding of God*, 293.
[58] See Lillback, ibid., 293f.
[59] Calvin, comm.. loc. cit., trans. John Owen, *Calvin's Commentaries* (Grand Rapids: Baker, vol. XIX, 1979), 447-48, italics added.

saw the potential of merit in the prelapsarian state, in which God was seen again to have "bound himself" to reward the obedience that his law as it was then articulated demanded.

While, then, "Calvin's theology permits no merit in the prelapsarian context,"[60] it is still the case that he saw the prelapsarian covenant connected with law, obedience, and conditional life. Lillback perceptively observes that the harmony of these positions in Calvin's thought turns on his "idea of greater and lesser grace." The Christian possesses the "greater grace" of perseverance. Adam possessed only "lesser grace," without perseverance. He was defectible. And if Adam had not fallen, it would be as a result of his obedience in this lesser grace, but, as Calvin resolves it, not due to *meritorious* obedience.

Our conclusion is threefold. First, Calvin did not hold to the presence of potential merit as intrinsic to the prelapsarian covenantal arrangements. In that respect he is followed by, for example, Turretin, Owen, and Murray. But we can concur with Lillback's finding that for Calvin "the basic significance of the covenant [was] the *binding of God* in sovereign humiliation with men, who are in turn bound to perform their duties of faith and obedience toward him."[61]

Second, the attribution of potential merit to our first parents' obedience entered theological thought explicitly in the post-Calvinian federal theology (arguably via Witsius, as cited), though not all subsequent Reformed theologians held to the presence of potential merit.

Third, we take note of Calvin's comment on Philippians 2:9, that while it is false to say "that Christ suffered upon the cross, that he might acquire *for himself, by the merit of his work*, what he did not possess," it is true that "he *merited*

---

[60] Lillback, *The Binding of God*, 299.
[61] Ibid., 307, italics added.

salvation for us."[62] It is precisely that *attainment of merit* that we have brought into focus when we have concluded that the substitutionary work of Christ was meritorious in the sense that he did for us in our fallen, Adamic state what we could not do for ourselves. In that, he earned and conveyed to us by gracious imputation the merit of which we stood in need, the merit that Adam could have acquired but did not. In that, again, the justice as well as the demands of the holiness of God are satisfied. Holding in view that the first Adam is typical of the Second, the claim of the absence of potential merit (and the claim that the reward would only have been by grace) from the first Adam would require it to be concluded that the Second Adam also was rewarded only by grace. In that event the claim that merit attached to the reward earned by the substitutionary work of Christ would be evacuated. Reformed theology would thereby be seriously damaged.

Finally, what is to be said, then, of the place of grace and of works of merit in the prelapsarian covenant? In short, God graciously bound himself to reward Adam's works of obedience. By an act of grace God surrendered his right by creation to require obedience without reward. God graciously promised reward. He thereby bound himself, in faithfulness to his own integrity, to that potential reward. A proper understanding of the earliest covenantal structure requires, we have argued, a due regard to the "works principle" that was inherent in it and which, in certain respects, was present also in the Mosaic administration of the covenant of grace. As was stated in the preceding text, God's establishing his covenantal promise was, in itself, an act of *grace*. His rewarding Adam for his obedience would have been an act of his *justice*. That, as we have seen the questions at issue, lies at the heart of the doctrine of the covenant of works.

It is of interest to note Karlberg's summary: "Once we

---

[62] Calvin, comm. loc. cit., trans. John Pringle, *Calvin's Commentaries* (Grand Rapids: Baker, vol. XXI, 1979), 59-60, italics added.

recognize and appreciate the full integrity of the biblical doctrine of the covenant of works as that which characterizes *the first relationship between the Creator and the creature*, we are prepared to consider the teaching of Scripture on the Mosaic Covenant as manifesting in some sense the features of the first covenant of works.... Outside of Christ, all stand guilty.... The covenant *whose principle of life-inheritance is that of works* can never be reinstituted. The operation of the *works-principle*, then, in the Mosaic Covenant cannot be interpreted so as to constitute the covenant under Moses as a covenant of works."[63] The thesis we have set out to defend in the foregoing chapter is reflected in Karlberg's concluding reference to "Christ's ultimate fulfillment of the covenant of works broken by Adam" and his final comment that "a repudiation of the biblical concept of works (the law-gospel distinction) destroys the doctrine of the atonement of Christ and justification by faith."[64]

---

[63] Karlberg, "Reformed Interpretation of the Mosaic Covenant," 54, italics added.
[64] Ibid., 57.

Chapter 4

The Status of the Will and the States of Human Consciousness

Augustine, in his complaint against Pelagius, saw that the implications of Adam's fall were to be traced to its effect on the will, the volitional faculty of the soul. That effect was both direct and indirect. At the Fall, the faculties of the soul, the mind, heart, and will, or the intellectual, emotion, and volitional faculties, were weakened and disabled. And the mind, having lost in its darkened condition its hegemony as the prince of the faculties, was no longer able to instruct the will to do that which was good. The sin by which our first parents fell from their initial state was their false assertion of autonomy against their Creator. That involved their repudiation of the covenantal obligations inherent in what we have discussed in the preceding chapters as the covenant of works. Our objective in this chapter is to examine at more length the implications of that primeval Fall as they bear on the understanding of the contemporary human condition. For that purpose, the status of the will, its freedom of function or otherwise as Augustine and Pelagius debated it, comes prominently into view.

The framers of the Westminster standards (1647) – of which, with progressive variations, the Savoy Declaration of Faith (1658) is the offspring and the Baptist Confession (1689) is the grandchild – judiciously addressed the subject of man's free will only after they had elaborated certain doctrines that are necessarily precedent. The latter were concerned with the being, the covenantal ordination, and the providence of God, along with the creation, the fall, and the salvability of man by the substitutionary, redemptive work of Christ. At the heart of the doctrinal complex that thereby comes into view is the relation between the two issues that have for centuries troubled philosophers, systematic theologians, and the ordinary Christian in the ordinary affairs of life. Those issues have to do with, first, the eternally wise, sovereign, and gracious predestination of God and his providential ordering of outcomes in the universe that he spoke into existence; and second, the responsibility for actions that rests, with equal conviction, on the persons whom God made in his image. If it is to be held that "God's works of providence are his most holy, wise, and powerful preserving and governing all his creatures, and all their actions,"[1] then the twofold question arises: What remains for significant decision and choice of action by man? And what, in the light of that, properly attaches to those actions as human responsibility? The question then follows whether a genuine and sustainable ethic, with ethical criteria and judgmental standards, attaches to human action.

The distinguished scientist, Albert Einstein, confronted the relation between divine sovereignty and human responsibility and his conclusion provides a backdrop to widespread opinion. "Nobody, certainly, will deny that the idea of the existence of an omnipotent, just, and omnibeneficent personal

---

[1] Westminster Shorter Catechism, Question 11.

God is able to accord man solace, help and guidance; also by virtue of its simplicity it is accessible to the most undeveloped mind. But ... if this being is omnipotent then every occurrence, including every human action, every human thought, and every human feeling and aspiration is also his work. How is it possible to think of holding men responsible for their deeds and thoughts before such an almighty Being?"[2] Einstein then, holding to what he saw as the "decisive weaknesses attached to this idea," recognized bluntly that "The main source of the present-day conflict between the spheres of religion and science lies in this concept of a personal God." His own refuge was that of the rationalist-pantheist philosopher, Spinoza (1632-1677), and with him he urged that we should think of the universe itself as God.[3] The modern British philosopher, Anthony Flew, addresses this nexus of questions and writes dismissively of "the scandalous doctrine of divine predestination."[4] Such is the drift of thought and the bequest that sophisticated opinion has made to common concern. The issue reduces, in its essence and basis, to whether we may hold securely to the existence and ordering of a personal God. The argument that follows will answer that question in the affirmative.

From the side of the theologians, the most important and probably the best known and most frequently cited contribution is the eighteenth-century work of Jonathan Edwards, *An Inquiry into ... [the] Freedom of the Will*. Edwards argues that the will is not capable of independently determining its own action. He forcibly rejects "the Arminian notion of freedom, that the will influences, orders, and determines itself."[5]

---

[2] A. Einstein, *Out of My Later Years* (New York: The Philosophical Library, 1950), 26-27, cited in Anthony Flew, *An Introduction to Western Philosophy: Ideas and Argument from Plato to Popper* (London: Thames and Hudson, 1989), 222.
[3] See Anthony Flew, idem, loc. cit.
[4] Ibid., 234.
[5] Edwards, op. cit., 45.

Rather, "every act of the will is some way connected with the understanding, and is as the greatest apparent good is."[6] "It is ... impossible for the will to choose contrary to its own ... preponderating inclination."[7] In short, there is, Edwards claims, no "freedom of will lying in the power of the will to determine itself,"[8] and the explanation of the action of the will as it exists by nature lies in "a certain deformity in the nature of the dispositions and acts of the heart."[9] Light is thrown on the whole question before us by Edwards' statement that the explanation of man's willing action is grounded in "the total depravity and corruption of man's nature, whereby his heart is wholly under the power of sin."[10] That is the source of man's "fixed bias and inclination."[11]

Edwards here confirms one of our principal conclusions that the will is not capable of independent, uninstructed action. He concludes, "Every act of the will is some way connected with the understanding." He is, in a strict sense, a necessitarian, in that "the acts of the will are none of them contingent in such a sense as to be without all necessity, or so as not to be necessary with a necessity of consequence and connexion."[12] That necessity and necessary connection exist because the actions of the will are determined by instructions received from the human faculties of mind and heart, the intellectual and emotional faculties of the soul. Edwards does provide in that connection a less than felicitous distinction between human natural ability and moral ability. It leads him to conceive of the status of the will as free, or as possessing a certain natural ability. That is so in the sense that it is, and it remains in the fallen state, freely capable of acting in response

---

[6] Ibid., 86.
[7] Idem, 73.
[8] Idem, 329.
[9] Idem, 341.
[10] Idem, 325.
[11] Idem, 321.
[12] Idem, 86.

to instruction, subject, of course, to the absence of external constraints or impediments. But against that natural ability, the moral ability is shackled by what he observed as the bias in the understanding.

The status of the question

It follows from these introductory observations that three possible positions regarding the freedom of the will warrant recognition and, in the present space, at least minimal investigation. First, it has been assumed by secular thought that no personal God exists and exerts any relation at all to the human person or the human will. That is the position of atheism which descends from the initial sin of Adam that made the false and damning assertion of autonomy from God. That false assertion was an assertion of metaphysical, epistemological, and ethical autonomy. The metaphysical assertion amounted to the effective denial of man's creaturehood, and it existed in the claim that man was not the responsible creature of a Creator-God. The epistemological assertion was the claim that man could discover all necessary criteria of truth in knowledge from within himself or from within the intramundane environment in which he had come to self-consciousness. No external or independent source of knowledge criteria was necessary or relevant to the human situation. The assertion of ethical autonomy was the claim that man could discover within himself, or again within the existing intramundane environment or in social opinion or whatever cultural complex existed, all necessary criteria of right action and behavior. In that sense it was claimed that the will was perfectly free, autonomous, and capable of independent action. That essential claim, that we might refer to as atheism proper, need not detain us unduly.

Second, a position of semi-autonomy, or, to the extent that it is properly understood, a denial of the true God as he has revealed himself and his relation with man, exists in the claims of the sub-biblical theology that informs a variety of non-Reformed and evangelical positions. Foremost among these, so far as it is presented as a form of evangelicalism, is Arminianism in one or the other of its semi-Pelagian forms. In those schemes of things, a personal God is understood to exist and man is, to varying degrees, understood to stand in a relation of responsibility and obligation to him. But again to varying degrees, inherent in such positions is a defective claim that originated in the early history of the church. That is that the will was substantially unaffected by the Fall. Man as he now exists, therefore, is free and freely able to accept or reject the offer of God's overtures of mercy to him. Such claims, advanced by Pelagius and controverted by the worthy Augustine in the fourth century, were again proposed by Pighius and countered by Calvin in the sixteenth century.[13] They came to prominence again in the Remonstrant theology that called forth the biblical-Reformed response of the Canons of Dordt in the seventeenth century.[14] The same division of belief and commitment led to the cleavage between Wesley and Whitefield and tarnished the testimony of the evangelical awakening in the eighteenth century.[15] The deviant doctrinal stance that such claims of autonomy or semi-autonomy involve continues to influence the testimony and preaching of large segments of evangelicalism at the present time. A neo-evangelical movement arose in the United States in the second half of the twentieth century, with such prominent persons as Carl F. H. Henry as its spokesman in the early days of the Journal, *Christianity Today*, Fuller Theological Seminary as

---

[13] John Calvin, *A Treatise on the Eternal Predestination of God* in *Calvin's Calvinism*, trans. Henry Cole (Grand Rapids: Eerdmans, 1956).
[14] See the outline in Beeke and Ferguson, eds., *Reformed Confessions Harmonized*.
[15] For the Wesley-Whitefield divergence, see Arnold Dallimore, *George Whitefield: The Life and Times of the Great Evangelist of the Eighteenth-Century Revival*, 1:307-19, 451-2.

its teaching institution, and Billy Graham as its prominent evangelist. It was, at least in its last-mentioned expression, decidedly Arminian in emphasis and it advanced the misguided assumptions of the autonomy of the will.

The third of the positions that warrant recognition is that of the Reformed expression of the biblical faith that rests its case on the reality of a personal God. It says, as the Westminster Shorter Catechism states it, that "The decrees of God are his eternal purpose, according to the counsel of his will, whereby, for his own glory, he hath foreordained whatsoever comes to pass."[16] The decrees of God are executed by his works of providence, superadded to his work of creation.[17]

Against the background of these observations it is possible to consider more precisely the states of human consciousness as they bear on the understanding of the status of the will. We shall look briefly at, first, man's prelapsarian state; secondly, the status of the will in man's fallen state as that was determined by the bequest of Adam's fall; and thirdly, the status of the will as it exists by virtue of the grace of regeneration that the Holy Spirit communicates to those whom Christ redeemed. Some comments will then follow on the implications of the relevant doctrine for the wider systematization of theology and for the practice of the Christian life.

The prelapsarian status of the will

The freedom of the will in man's prelapsarian state is implicit in the fact that he was created as the image of God.[18] We shall refer in due course to the relation of the will of man in its created state of freedom to the necessities of God's eternal ordination. That important issue has already been raised by

---

[16] Westminster Shorter Catechism, Question 7.
[17] Ibid., Question 8.
[18] The meaning and implications of that fact are explored in Vickers, *Christian Confession*, Chap. 3.

the objections of atheism, and we shall return to the doctrinal necessities that arise in that connection. As to man's initial condition, Turretin noted that the probationary directive that God gave to Adam, that he should not eat of the tree of the knowledge of good and evil, was itself "necessary ... to declare that man was created by him [God] with free will; for if he had been without it, he would not have imposed such a law upon him."[19] The Westminster Shorter Catechism similarly states that it was when they were "left to the freedom of their own will" that our first parents "fell from the estate wherein they were created."[20]

"In his state of innocency," as the Westminster Confession puts it, the will of man possessed a "natural liberty,"[21] meaning that the will was not forced to good or evil by any external necessity. That statement and fact are reflected in what we shall refer to as the distinction between "free will" and "free agency," as they characterize the status of the will in man's fallen state. What Edwards had in view as his "natural ability" as opposed to "moral ability" reflects the same fact, that the will is free in the sense in which it is not subject to external constraints or necessities. But a singularly important theological doctrine is to be engaged at that point.

In his original state, and in the light of the initially-established freedom of his will, our first parent stood in a state of *posse non peccare* (possible not to sin). It was possible for him not to sin and fall from the state of blessedness in which he had been created. Adam possessed all endowments, including the freedom and strength of will, necessary to enable him to continue in a state of beatitude, to maintain his state of intrinsic holiness and rectitude and communion with God, and to obtain by his obedience the full blessing of eternal life that God had conditionally promised to him. That

---
[19] Turretin, *Elenctic Theology*, 1:580.
[20] Westminster Shorter Catechism, Question 13.
[21] Westminster Confession, IX, I-II.

promise was conveyed in the terms of the covenant of works. It carried with it a twofold prospect. First, Adam, by merit of his work of obedience to the law of God, would be rewarded with the blessing of benediction and confirmation in the moral state of holiness. The law that conveyed that promise was inherent in Adam's consciousness by reason of his creation as the image of God, and it was communicated to him more fully when, in the form of the Second Person of the Godhead, God walked with him in the garden in the cool of the day (Gen. 3:8). But secondly, by his disobedience to that clearly communicated law, Adam would merit the curse and malediction which did, in fact, fall upon him. While Adam was, as has been said, *posse non peccare*, his fall, which implicated by immediate imputation all those descending from him by ordinary generation,[22] placed us all in a position of *non posse non peccare* (not possible not to sin).

The more complete understanding of the status of the will in the prelapsarian state is assisted by a recognition of the state of the faculties of the soul as they initially existed in their intrapersonal relation. The mind, or the intellectual faculty, naturally knew God and responded with clarity and uncluttered reason to the knowledge that was inherent in Adam's created condition. Adam naturally knew God, he knew the joys and benefits of communion with God, and he knew what God required of him in order that his pristine state might be preserved. He could by that means anticipate the eternal life which God had promised on condition of obedience. That knowledge, existent within the range of a purity of mind and untarnished intellectual rectitude, was confirmed by the sacraments that inhered in Adam's initial state. Those sacraments included, in addition to the Sabbath that prefigured the eternal Sabbath of rest, the privilege of partaking of the tree of life. That was of particular sacramental significance. In his partaking of that tree, Adam was reminded of,

---

[22] Westminster Shorter Catechism, Question 16.

and he thereby received the confirmation of the prospect of the eternal blessing that God had conditionally promised. It was a sacramental confirmation of God's faithfulness to his promise. That sacrament, the privilege of eating of the tree of life, was, of course, denied to Adam after he had fallen. The cherubims were set to guard the entrance to the garden lest our first parents should try to take of the tree, thereby again partaking of a sacrament for which they were now no longer qualified (Gen. 3:24). Their doing so would have heaped greater damnation on themselves, and the parallel with the danger of partaking of the sacrament of the Lord's Supper unworthily at the present time will be clear (1 Cor. 11:29).

At the same time, with the heart or the emotional faculty Adam naturally loved God, and that natural disposition, the *habitus* implicit in the soul, moved our first parent to love the law of God and to love the work of obedience. Coming to issue, then, is the fact that the mind or the intellectual faculty that naturally knew the law of God, and the heart or the emotional faculty that naturally loved God, naturally and in a harmonious concurrence instructed the will or the volitional faculty to obey God. In the pristine state the will did not act independently or determine its own action in separation from, and in distinction or autonomy from, the faculties of intellect and emotion. In the initial state of man there existed a harmony among the faculties. There was no discordance or possibility of disruption so long as the initial state of righteousness was preserved. And in that pristine state the mind was the prince of the faculties of the soul.[23]

In the fallen state of the soul a sorry reversal of those two pristine relations occurred. As a result of the Fall, the har-

---

[23] That original state of harmony among the faculties is observed by Turretin in his comment that man as created was characterized by "wisdom in the mind, holiness in the will, and rectitude in the affections. It bespeaks ... a *harmony* among the faculties" (italics added), *Elenctic Theology*, 1:466

mony of the faculties was shattered and the hegemony of the mind was displaced by that of the heart or the emotional faculty. That is clear from the way in which the apostle stated it to the Romans, when he observed that man is now by nature a "God-hater" (Rom. 1:30). Such is the sorry state to which all of mankind have fallen in Adam. At issue on a larger doctrinal canvas are the related issues of, first, the realities of the immediate imputation to us all of the guilt of Adam's first sin, and secondly, the transmission to us of the fallen nature that resulted from that sin.[24]

It follows that the confessional statement is correct, that notwithstanding his *posse non peccare*, man as created was mutable, and it was possible for him to fall. Though he was in his initial state in possession of certain of the communicable attributes of God,[25] he had not been granted the incommunicable attributes of impeccability or immutability. It will be seen in what follows that in his redeemed, regenerate state, man is now raised to a position in which it is impossible for him to fall, in the sense that it is impossible for him now to be disjoined from the union with Christ in which he has been established. It is in that carefully defined sense that the new

---

[24] In a larger study than our present space permits, extensive attention would be given to the critical and central doctrine of the imputation of Adam's sin. Two issues are involved in the doctrine of sin: first, the imputation of the guilt of Adam's first sin; and second, the transmission to "all those descending from him by ordinary generation" (Westminster Shorter Catechism, Question 16) of a sinful nature. The *locus classicus* of the discussion of these issues is contained in John Murray, *The Imputation of Adam's Sin* (Grand Rapids: Eerdmans, 1959), where Murray establishes the biblical doctrine of the *immediate*, as against the contrary supposition of *mediate*, imputation of sin. That says that no fact situation or condition, such as the possession of a fallen nature, mediated between Adam's first sin and the imputation of the guilt of it to all of Adam's posterity, of whom he was the representative or federal head.

[25] That aspect of the created state is discussed at length in Vickers, *Christian Confession*, chap. 3.

person's state of union with Christ is one of *non posse peccare*. Of course he can and he does sin. That is not at issue in our immediate discussion. But he cannot sin to the effect that he can be dislodged from the eternally secure state in which God has now established him in Christ (1 John 3:9).

The status of the will in man's fallen state

In the consideration of man's fallen state the implications of what has just been said come to their most pointed relevance. Now, in the state of sin, the mind is no longer able to know God for who he is in his gracious identity and to know the good which God had placed before mankind. And the heart is no longer able to love and naturally seek after the good. The mind and the heart, therefore, are no longer able to instruct the will to do the good. That disability of the soul in its fallen condition was well remarked by Luther in his debate with Erasmus at the time of the Reformation. "What can the will pursue," he asks, "when reason can propose to it nothing but the darkness of its own blindness and ignorance? Where reason is in error, and the will turned away, what good can man attempt or perform?"[26] In his state of sin, man is totally disabled from knowing, loving, and obeying God. That is simply because, as the apostle to the Gentiles has explained, man is now enslaved to the devil. "The god of this world," Paul explained, "hath blinded the mind" (2 Cor. 4:4), and "the natural man receiveth not the things of the Spirit of God; for they are foolishness unto him: neither can he know them, because they are spiritually discerned" (1 Cor. 2:14). Again on a larger doctrinal canvas than we are inspecting at present, man is described by the Scriptures as now existing in a state of total depravity. All of the faculties of the soul, the mind, the heart, and the will, are disabled from performing their initially-created functions and offices. That carries with it a

---

[26] Luther, *The Bondage of the Will*, 281.

number of doctrinal implications and implications for the life of man in sin.

First, as our confessional statements declare, "Man, by his fall into a state of sin, hath wholly lost all ability of will to any spiritual good accompanying salvation; so as, a natural man, being altogether averse from that good, is not able, by his own strength, to convert himself, or to prepare himself thereunto."[27] The soul's enslavement to the devil, the "strong man armed" that "keepeth his palace, his goods [the sinner comfortably asleep in his subjugation to sin] in peace" (Luke 11:21), makes his state one of irrevocable perdition unless the Spirit of God in regeneration should come with new enlightenment to him. Only when, as our Lord goes on to say in the same passage, "a stronger than he shall come upon him [the devil] and overcome him ... and divideth his spoils," can a person again know the life in God from which he had fallen. That occurs by the grace of God when "God, who commanded the light to shine out of darkness [at the first creation] has shined in our hearts, to give the light of the knowledge of the glory of God in the face of Jesus Christ" (2 Cor. 4:6).

Second, the distinction between what is to be referred to as free will on the one hand, and free agency on the other, now comes to pointed relevance. When the confession properly states that by his fall man "lost all ability of will to any spiritual good," it is saying, in the strictest sense of the term, that at the fall man lost his free will.[28] But while that is so, free agency remains. That means that man as he now exists is free to do that which is consistent with his nature. That, of course, is true of all God's creatures. A horse is free to act consistently with its nature as a horse. A cow is free to

---

[27] Westminster Confession, IX, III.
[28] Cunningham observes in that connection that "Calvin repeatedly quotes with approbation the striking and pithy saying of Augustine, that man, by making a bad use of his free will, lost both himself and it," *Historical Theology*, 1:578.

be consistently a cow. Each is free to act consistently with its nature, apart again from externally imposed constraints, a matter that need not detain us further, either in the case of man or animals. Again, the same applies to man as he now exists. He, too, is free to act consistently with his nature. But that nature is a sinful nature, and the lamentable result is that man is free only to be sinful. He can only act sinfully. Our Lord himself said clearly, "Whosoever committeth sin is the servant [or the slave] of sin" (John. 8:34). And he went on to state to the Jews who had demurred from his teaching that "Ye are of your father the devil, and the lusts of your father ye will do" (John 8:44). The apostle to the Romans said the same thing, "To whom ye yield yourselves servants [or slaves] to obey, his servants [slaves] ye are" (Rom. 6:16). Thus, the natural enslavement to Satan and sin means and implies that man in that state is no longer free. He naturally loves his sin. He is not free to obey God because he has no love for God. He is, in Paul's expressive terms, a God-hater. That is the alarming reality inherent in the loss of the freedom of the will that the Fall implied.

The natural free agency, that places a man in sin far below his pristine state of free will, is clarified by the apostle Peter when he adduces in his second epistle the proverb, "As a dog returneth to his vomit, so a fool returneth to his folly" (Prov. 26:11). Peter applies the proverb to explain the state of man in sin with an analogy to a sow: "the sow that was washed [returns to] her wallowing in the mire" (2 Peter 2:22). The unfortunate situation is that one may take a sow and wash her and clean her up in a manner quite inconsistent with her true nature and character. But then all one will have at that stage is a prettied-up sow. As soon as opportunity permits, she will return to her character and to the mire, her natural habitat. The poor creature was never anything but a sow. So it is with the sinner. No renovation other than the regenerating grace of God can change his or her character. The sinner is free only to be a sinner, apart from the renewing grace of God.

Third, the total depravity that characterizes the human situation as a result of the Fall means that all of the faculties of the soul are affected. Each of the faculties is disabled from performing its initial, harmonious, and God-honoring function. We have said that the will is disabled from obeying God and doing the "good" by reason that the intellectual and emotional faculties are no longer able to communicate to the will instructions to do the good. But that is not the end of the matter. The will, whatever might have been its initially-endowed strength and ability to act, is now in itself weakened. It is at that point that Edwards' "natural ability" as opposed to "moral ability" is doctrinally imprecise. It is not clear in Edwards' treatise on the will that he takes adequate account, not only of the dependence of the will on the preceding determination of the mind, but of the fact that the volitional faculty is itself weakened by the effects of the Fall.[29] For the status of the will as it exists after the Fall is clarified in the confessional statement that "Man, by his fall into a state of sin, hath *wholly lost all ability of will* to any spiritual good accompanying salvation."[30] "Hence the necessity," Cunningham observes, "not only of the conviction of sin and the illumination of the understanding, but also of the renovation of the will, in order to men's embracing Christ."[31] The will needs to be renewed and strengthened in and by the power that God conveys in the grace of regeneration. It is for that reason said that "Thy people shall be willing in the day of thy power" (Ps. 110:3); or as another translation has it, "Your people will offer themselves freely on the day of your power" (ESV). A new freedom, a new willingness, a new strength of will is endowed on and within the soul by the power of God

---

[29] Compare Cunningham's evaluation of Edwards' distinction between natural and moral inability and his objection to its adequacy in *Historical Theology*, 1:600-605.

[30] Westminster Confession, IX,III, italics added.

[31] Cunningham, *Historical Theology*, 1:621. See Turretin, *Elenctic Theology*, 1:675, Tenth topic, Q. 4, XIX.

when he declares his power by the regenerating work of his Holy Spirit. The meaning of the Catechism should impress us at that point when it says that "Effectual calling is the work of God's Spirit, whereby, convincing us of our sin and misery, enlightening our minds in the knowledge of Christ, *and renewing our wills*, he doth persuade *and enable* us to embrace Jesus Christ freely offered to us in the gospel."[32] In the regenerating work of the Spirit both an "enlightening of the mind" and a "renewing of the will" occur.

Fourth, a contemporary and erroneous doctrine has infiltrated the church and attempted to bolster the claim to free will by attacking the very doctrine of the knowledge of God, or the doctrine of the knowledge that God himself possesses. We should note its relevance. We have said that in the state of sin a person's will is disabled by reason of the lack of true knowledge and the darkness of understanding that has disabled the mind. But the lack of knowledge, the new and erroneous doctrine claims, cannot have the relevance for which we have argued, because in an important respect a lack of knowledge exists in God also. That lack of knowledge refers to processes and eventuation yet to occur in the history of the world. Startling as that claim is, it is, in its current incarnation, the reintroduction to the theology of the church of the old heresy of Socinianism that flourished in the sixteenth and seventeenth centuries. It is now being said that God does not know the future of the universe and of the people he has created and established in that universe. God, too, it is now claimed, must wait to discover the future eventuation in the universe which, as the biblical revelation insists, he spoke into being and which operates in accordance with God-created laws. That point has been made by Cunningham in stating that the Socinians "admit indeed that God knows all things that are knowable; but then they contend that future contingent events, such as the future actions of responsible agents, are not knowable,– do not come within the scope of what may be

---

[32] Westminster Shorter Catechism, Question 31, italics added.

known, even by an infinite Being; and, upon this ground, they allege that it is no derogation from the omniscience of God, that He does not, and cannot, know what is not knowable."[33]

That reintroduction of Socinian theology is a degeneration in doctrine beyond Arminianism. The latter scheme of things understands that God does, in fact, know the future. He thereby knows what every man, in the autonomous exercise of his free will, will do and will decide. God knows what human decisions and choices will be in, for example, the choice as to whether or not an individual will accept the offer of salvation which, as Arminianism maintains, Christ purchased for every man and which God now offers to him. Indeed, it is on the grounds of that foreknowledge of individuals' perfectly free action and choice, it is mistakenly claimed, that God elects certain people to eternal salvation. That divine choice is based on the grounds of individuals' sovereignly chosen belief in Christ. The neo-Socinianism now being referred to, which goes under such names as "Open Theism," moves beyond that erroneous belief. It claims that even God does not know the future, because that future is in no sense the subject of God's eternal ordination and decree. If, then, God is ignorant, and if God must wait to discover and to be surprised by what might occur, then man also is free to discover what might eventuate; and in that freedom nothing exists to influence or determine his action or the decision processes of his will. The Socinian scheme claims, in other words, that there is a complete indifference in the will of man as he now exists, an indifference that makes him free of all necessity or divine influence. Open Theism has been effectively discussed and responded to by a number of evangelical and Reformed authors.[34]

---

[33] Cunningham, *Historical Theology,* 2:173. For a futher discussion of the parallels between Socinianism and open theism see Robert B. Strimple, "What Does God Know?" in John H. Armstrong, ed., *The Coming Evangelical Crisis: Current Challenges to the Authority of Scripture and the Gospel* (Chicago: Moody, 1996), 140-41.

[34] See, for example, R. K. McGregor Wright, *No Place for Sovereignty:*

Fifth, notwithstanding the Fall, man continues to be the image of God.[35] He is still an immortal, rational, spiritual, moral, and speaking person. As that image, he retains his logical facility. Thus, the laws of logic are the same for the believer and the unbeliever. And it is undoubtedly the case that in many fields of learning the unregenerate person can and does know and think beyond the regenerate individual. As to the formal processes of logical thought, by reason of the common grace of God the unbeliever is often able to think through issues and problem situations as well as the believer. That does not mean that regeneration does not carry with it a new level of clarity of thought. Of course it may and does. But on a purely formal level the unregenerate person may be able to see and reason through the argument for the truth of Christianity that the believer may put to him. It may be asked in the light of that why, then, does not the unbeliever accept the truth of the argument that he is able logically to follow. Why, in other words, is the will not activated to turn to Christ, in whom alone are hid all the treasures of wisdom and knowledge (Col. 2:3)? It has already been stated that the impediment that stands in the way of the acceptance of the truth is what Jonathan Edwards referred to as the "bias" in the soul – the internal and moral constraint imposed on the will, and the hatred of God that Paul referred to eloquently in Romans 1.[36] The will, it is implied, is not an originative faculty of the soul. The action of the will emanates from the originative instructions of the intellectual and emotional faculties.

What's Wrong with Freewill Theism (Downers Grove, Ill.: InterVarsity Press, 1996); John Frame, *No Other God: A Response to Open Theism* (Phillipsburg: P&R, 2001), noting 32-36 and references cited for a recognition of Socinianism; John Piper et.al., eds., *Beyond the Bounds* (Wheaton, Ill.: Crossway Books, 2003).
[35] See the fuller discussion in Vickers, *Christian Confession*, chap. 3 regarding the formal faculties of soul in the unregenerate person.
[36] The subject of the status of the will in the aspects we are here addressing is treated by Turretin in *Elenctic Theology*, 1:659ff.

The faculties of the soul

We have spoken of the faculties of the soul and of the dependence of the will on the functioning and instructions of the mind and the heart. That dependence continues in the fallen state of sin. In its weakened state the will continues to depend on the preferences and the vision of what Edwards referred to as the "greatest apparent good."[37] The conception of that good is again transmitted to the will by the mind and the heart. The difference that now exists is that the hegemony of the mind has been displaced by that of the heart or the emotional faculty. A divergence of view has appeared in the historical literature, however, regarding the faculties of the soul, and as a result a divergence of understanding of the points we have made in that respect may arise.

Conrad Cherry, in his valuable study of Edwards' theology, discusses the respects in which Edwards argued against the rationalist Arminianism of Charles Chauncy. Chauncy, Cherry concludes, "is a captive of the scholastic psychology which breaks human agency into *related but separate* faculties."[38] Cherry goes on to argue that Edwards rejected that "scholastic faculty psychology." That last statement means that Edwards rejected the claim that the faculties of the soul were capable of autonomous, uninstructed activity *separately considered and in their separate and independent action.* Edwards rejected that claim because he understood the will to be subject to the precedent instructions of the mind. But at that point a unique perspective of Edwards' is worthy of note. As he saw things, "The will, and the affections of the soul, are not two faculties (and) the affections are no other than the more vigorous and sensible exercises of the inclination and will of the soul."[39] Edwards follows Calvin in the latter's

---

[37] Edwards, *Freedom of the Will*, 86.
[38] Cherry, *Theology of Jonathan Edwards*, 167, italics added.
[39] Edwards, *The Religious Affections* (Edinburgh: Banner of Truth,

statement that "the human soul consists of two faculties, understanding and will."[40] Calvin continues in the same context, agreeing with our proposition regarding the precedence of the mind, that "the understanding is ... the leader and governor of the soul; and that the will is always mindful of the bidding of the understanding ... the understanding now governs the direction of the will." While we are not here concerned with a mere counting of the faculties of the soul, it is important to bring to adequate focus the status of the soul, and of the capacity for action of the will within it, as that is determined by the place and function of the affections or the emotional faculty.

That is particularly important now that the affections are to be seen as predominant over the intellect in determining actions in the state of sin. Calvin, speaking in the same context of man as created, anticipates the statement we have adduced by referring to Adam's "right understanding" and "affections," observing that "the primary seat of the divine image was in the *mind and heart*." In that primeval state, Calvin observes further, Adam "had his *affections* kept within the bounds of reason."[41] In one way or another, then, cognizance is given to the affective faculty or capacity of the soul.

Having in view the application of that understanding of the soulish faculties to what is now the fallen condition of man, it is of note that in Philippians 4:7 Paul draws the distinction we have in view in his reference to "hearts and minds." The Puritan commentator, Matthew Poole, refers at that point to "affections and reasoning." Calvin at the same point, while maintaining his claim that "Scripture is accustomed to divide the soul of man, as to its frailties [faculties?], into two parts – the *mind* and the *heart*," comments that "The *mind* means the *understanding*, while the *heart* denotes all the

---

1961), 24-25.
[40] Calvin, *Institutes*, 1:194.
[41] Idem, 188, italics added.

dispositions or *inclinations*."⁴² But it is of interest in this connection to take note of the apostle's statement in Romans 6:17, where he says, "ye obeyed from the heart that form of doctrine." Involved in the action of the believer, Paul is saying there, was the action of the will, or the volitional faculty of the soul ("ye obeyed"), the heart or the emotional faculty ("from the heart"), and the mind or the intellectual faculty ("that form of doctrine"). Martyn Lloyd-Jones has grasped that concurrence and conjunction of the faculties of the soul clearly in his exposition of the text.⁴³ Edwards, moreover, though he subsumes the affections under the activity of the will as already indicated,⁴⁴ appears to take account of the wider faculty designation we have adopted in his *Charity and its Fruits,* where he states that "a man has a *heart* and an *understanding*, and a *will*."⁴⁵

Given, then, the capacities of the soul as they exist in man in his fallen condition, the question that comes critically to focus is that of the activity of the will in the process of the sinner's conversion and his rescue by the grace of God from the entailment of sin in which Adam's fall had placed him.

The status and capacity of the will in the regenerate state

It is beyond the scope of our present discussion to examine at length the meaning of the apostolic statement, "By grace are ye saved through faith; and that not of yourselves; it is the gift of God" (Eph. 2:8). The gospel is the gospel of the grace of God. Salvation is by grace, and it is by grace in all of its parts. God has made Christ to be to the sinner whom Christ redeemed "wisdom and righteousness and sanctification and

---

⁴² Calvin, Comm. loc. cit.
⁴³ See D. M. Lloyd-Jones, *Romans: An Exposition of Chapter 6, The New Man* (London: Banner of Truth, 1972), 208ff.
⁴⁴ See also Edwards, *The Religious Affections*, 198.
⁴⁵ Edwards, *Charity and its Fruits* (Edinburgh: Banner of Truth, 1969), 58, italics added. See also Calvin, *Institutes*, 1:284.

redemption" (1 Cor. 1:30). The terms of the gospel are spread liberally over the pages of the Scriptures and the gospel is evacuated of its meaning by any diminution of the grace of God that accomplishes and applies redemption. It is of the essence of the Reformed articulation of the Christian faith to insist that it is the grace of God that is the *efficient* cause of salvation, the substitutionary life and sacrifice of Jesus Christ is the *meritorious* cause, and faith, the *instrumental* cause. But it is beyond our immediate scope to speak at length of the operation of the grace of God in the process of conversion. If it were otherwise, we should make clear what is to be understood as the prevenient grace of God and the preparatory work of the Holy Spirit in the soul of the sinner. That may proceed even to advanced length and degree as the letter to the Hebrews tells us (Heb. 6), and it may or may not, depending on the sovereign decree of God, culminate in the Spirit's conveyance to an individual of the grace of regeneration. It would then be necessary to speak in that context of the meaning of the reciprocal imputation that is involved in God's declarative statement of the sinner's forensic justification – the imputation of the guilt of the sinner's sin to Christ in his substitutionary sacrifice and the imputation of the righteousness of Christ to the sinner. But from the context in which those vital issues of doctrine might be more fully discussed, our focus at this point is confined to the different but relevant question of what is to be understood as the place and function of the human will in the process of salvation.

The import of that question is clarified by noting at the outset three possible answers that might be given in the light of positions taken as to the status of the will. If, in the first place, legitimacy were accorded the claims of Arminianism or the Remonstrant theology, it would be said that the human will as it now stands is free and able to embrace or reject in an autonomous sense the offer of the gospel. Or again, on a larger doctrinal canvas than the present space permits, distinctions might be drawn between the starkest claims of Pelagianism and other sympathetic systems of semi-Pelagianism. In the former, the will, not having been disabled by the Fall, is assumed to be completely capable of accepting or rejecting at any time whatever overtures of God's grace it encounters. The will in that scheme of things is free from divine control or assistance in the fullest and most complete sense. In lesser forms, such as the Arminian scheme proposes, the human will is active in the process of salvation and works in cooperation with divine grace.[46] In effect, these sub-biblical schemes advance what we have already referred to as *autosoterism* on the one hand, or *synergism* on the other. The first of those terms implies that in the final analysis, by reason of the assumed freedom of the will, the sovereignty of decision as to whether the gospel invitation to Christ will be accepted or rejected resides completely in the hands of the individual person. In its starkest form, it is the individual who sovereignly determines his own salvation. God is robbed of his sovereign prerogatives. In that event, man saves himself. Salvation is then an autosoterism.

If, as in semi-Pelagian forms of errant theological doctrines at this point, it were supposed that salvation depends on a cooperation between the grace of God and a human will that is free to a greater or lesser extent, then a form of *synergism* would be held. But it is announced with clarity by the Word of God that because the human will in the state of sin is bound and enslaved to the devil and is shackled by the disabilities of sin, the will is totally disabled from any possibility of cooperation with divine grace. Salvation, then, cannot be said to be an *autosoterism* or a *synergism*. Salvation, as we have concluded earlier, is a *divine monergism*. If the Scritpural expla-

---

[46] Turretin, in *Elenctic Theology*, 2:542ff., illumines this important area of doctrine by asking, "Whether in the first moment of conversion man is merely passive or whether his will cooperates in some measure with the grace of God. The former we affirm and deny the latter against all synergists."

nation of the status of the will in the state of sin that results from the Fall is understood, there can be no other explanation of salvation except that it is in all its parts the effect of the sovereign regenerating grace of God.

It is of critical importance to understand what that conclusion does not say. We are not saying that the faculties of the soul are inactive in the process of salvation. We are simply saying, in accord with Scripture, that the faculties are not engaged in any *meritorious* respect. The sense in which the faculties are active must be understood to be consistent with all that has been said regarding the disabilities and bondage of the faculties in sin. The fact that the appeal of the gospel comes to the sinner with its command to repent (Acts 17:30; Matt. 4:17) and to believe on the Lord Jesus Christ (Acts 16:31) means that the first appeal of the gospel is to the mind. The fact that man is still, notwithstanding his fallen state, the image of God, a rational, spiritual, moral person, means that he is capable of following the logical statements that explain his sinful condition, his obligations to his Creator, his prospect of eternal perdition, and the realities of Christ's atonement for sin. The sinner is, then, capable of seeing the logic of what the gospel announces. And if it should fall within the compass of divine predestination to bring the sinner to salvation, the Holy Spirit will awaken the mind and the heart of that sinner to see the deeper salvific meaning of what now confronts him. That will then be seen, not only in the logical sense of a sequence of assimilable statements, but as an illuminated command to repent that produces the sinner's flight to Christ. The mind of the unregenerate person is engaged in that respect. If that were not so, then what the Scriptures have revealed as the meaning of integral personhood would be negated.

The work of the Holy Spirit within the soul, like the wind that blows where it wishes (John 3:8) in mysterious ways that are beyond our capacity to corral and understand, will engage and move the emotional faculty of the soul. The will is then moved to embrace Jesus Christ. The process of salvation is then such that it issues in a whole-souled response to the gospel. That is the outcome that the Puritan fathers wisely articulated when they wrote, "Effectual calling is the work of God's Spirit, whereby, convincing us of our sin and misery enlightening our minds in the knowledge of Christ [the operation on and within the mind or the intellectual faculty], and renewing our wills [the operation on and within the volitional faculty] he doth persuade and enable us to embrace Jesus Christ [the volitional faculty in action and the engagement of the emotional faculty] freely offered to us in the gospel."[47] The will in itself suffered a weakening at the Fall, concomitant with the depravity of the other faculties, and the will also, in itself, needs to be renewed in regeneration. Then the renewed and strengthened will is in a state to accept and act upon the directions of the renewed mind and heart. In short, the prevenient grace of God works by his Spirit in the faculties of the soul of the sinner, it makes its appeal to the sinner via the capacities of those faculties, and it may or may not, depending on God's sovereign purpose, culminate in conveying to the sinner the grace of regeneration and moving the will to turn to Christ. In the latter case, but only at that point, is the will again freed to move in repentance to Christ. It is then, but only then, that the will is again free. The shackles of Satanic enslavement have been removed and free will has been reestablished in the soul.

That is so by virtue of the meaning and effects of the Holy Spirit's work of regeneration in the soul. By that sovereign work, the faculties of the soul are endowed with abilities and capacities they did not previously possess, and a new disposition or principle of action, a new *habitus*, is created in the soul.

Two final points are to be made. First, it follows from all that has been said of the bondage of the will in the state of sin

---

[47] Westminster Shorter Catechism, Question 31.

that regeneration by the grace of God is in the fullest sense prior to faith and conversion. In the context of our present discussion regarding the state of the will, it follows that regeneration is prior to the freedom of the will. That critical fact is brought to focus again by a consideration of the contrary claims of the Pelagian and semi-Pelagian systems of doctrine. In the Arminian scheme, for example, its claim for the relative freedom of the will means that faith and belief in Christ are placed before regeneration. One is born again, regenerated, it is said, because and as a result of the expression of faith in Christ. Regeneration then turns on the competence of a prior expression of faith. But such a doctrinal construction flies in the face of all that has been said regarding the disabilities and the bondage of the will that characterize the state of sin. On the contrary, the declaration of the gospel is that those, and only those, will turn to Christ in repentance and faith who have been made regenerate by the grace of God. Regeneration is prior to faith. Regeneration is prior to the freedom of the will.

Second, what, then, is to be said of the status of the will in the state of salvation in which, having been born again and received by adoption into the family of God, the individual works out by God's grace the process of sanctification? The renewed faculties of the soul – the enlightened mind that knows in new ways the law of God, the newly enlivened heart that loves God and the righteous law of God, and the renewed and strengthened will that strains to follow and obey God – are jointly engaged in pursuing the holiness to which God has called that individual in Christ. The renewed faculties are now freed to function toward that end with a reestablished concurrence and harmony. That means that a whole-souled engagement of mind, heart, and will now determines the new-born person's progress through this life to the promised inheritance in Christ that awaits him (Heb. 9:15). But we are not saying that the will at that stage, or at any stage in this life, is perfectly free from sin. It is beyond our immediate scope to speak of the interruptions to the process of sanctification that can and do occur in the life of the Christian.[48] What is being said is that in the condition of salvation the will has been renewed to a new freedom. That is what is at issue in the question as to the status of the will in the redeemed people of God. "When God converts a sinner ... he freeth him from his natural bondage under sin; by his grace alone, enables him *freely to will* and to do that which is spiritually good."[49]

The work of regeneration in the soul that elevates the will to a new freedom does not imply that God has thereby communicated to the will the attribute of perfect immutability. That is so because of what is implied in the possibility of remaining acts of sin in the life of the Christian. But at the same time it is true that the will in its renewed state, supported and carried along as it is by the inner and secret working of the will of God (Phil. 2:12-13), now sees before it the responsibility to pursue holiness "without which no man shall see the Lord" (Heb. 12:14). By the grace of God the will now lifts the experience of the person to new levels of obedience and realization of the blessing of God. If that were not so, the lie would be given to the entire engagement that the blessed third Person of the Godhead, the Holy Spirit, undertook in the predeterminate council of the Godhead before the foundation of the world. For there he willingly undertook the redemptive office and assignment of applying to those for whom Christ died the benefits and blessings that Christ purchased for them in his substitutionary atonement. It is the assigned office of the Holy Spirit to conduct such persons to glory.

Finally, it is the prospect, as the confession states it, that "The will of man is made perfectly and immutably free to do good alone, in the state of glory only."[50]

---

[48] That important question is addressed in the Westminster Confession, IX, IV.
[49] Idem, italics added.
[50] Westminster Confession, IX, V.

Conclusion

Three conclusions follow. First, philosophic opinion, as observed in the claims of the scientist Albert Einstein and the philosopher Anthony Flew, sees an irreconcilable conflict, in theory and in fact, between the biblical revelation of a sovereign personal God and the freewill responsibilities of man. Sophisticated opinion-makers, therefore, will have nothing to do with the notion, as they see it, of a personal God. In the light, on the contrary, of the biblical explanation of the status of the will in the successive states of human consciousness, the conclusion follows that man in the exercise of all of his faculties, notably in the present context the exercise of will, is dependent on the grace of the personal God. That grace of God is operative not only in the believer's rescue from the state of sin and his justification, but in, as we have seen, all parts and stages of his progress in sanctification. The doctrinal triad of creation, fall, and redemption speak eloquently to that reality throughout the entire pages of divine revelation.

But a further point is relevant to that claim and will bear on our conclusion regarding the mystery of God's ordination in relation to man's responsibility of will. It is to be held in mind in that connection that the fact that *God is*, that he is a personal God, and that he has revealed himself to the rational creatures he made in his image is the only sustainable and productive starting point in all of our theology and our Christian apologetic. Our approach to truth, and certainly in the present instance our claims as to the status of the will, emanate from what is involved in our transcendental apologetic. A "transcendental" system of thought is one that proceeds from an initial laying down of the conditions that must be satisfied for any instance of knowledge to be possible. Our apologetic is transcendental in that it is only because, as our initial postulate states, *God is,* that any meaning at all, on any level of enquiry, is possible. The meaning of any fact or fact situation in the world or in human life is true and attainable by human investigation only because God thought all the facts before the foundation of the world. He spoke them into existence, and he sustains them by God-created laws of being and operation. As Van Til has stated, "The absolutely certain proof of the truth of Christianity is that unless its truth is presupposed there is no proof of anything. Christianity is proved as being the very foundation of the idea of proof itself."[51]

Second, the position we have taken regarding the status of the will implies a rejection of all claims to human autonomy, whether those claims are made in their metaphysical, epistemological, or ethical connotations. We have rejected all theological-doctrinal systems that suggest that the process of the salvation of sinners is in any sense an autosoterism or a synergism. Salvation is only, always, and completely the sovereign accomplishment of the grace of God set forth in Christ and ministered by his Holy Spirit. As to the capacities for action of the human will, we have rejected a number of theologically errant suggestions. The will, the volitional faculty of the soul, is not capable of determining its own action. It cannot and does not function with autonomy from, and in separation from, other faculties of the soul. It is weakened and disabled in the natural state of sin unless and until it is renewed and strengthened by the effectual calling of God.

Third, those conclusions cannot be sustained apart from a final implication of our rejection of the philosophers' complaint with which we started. How, in short, is the apparent conflict between the sovereignty of a personal God and the action and responsibility of the human will to be breached? Is there any response from the Christian apologetic that can ease, if not resolve, that apparent problem? Our answer is twofold. First, as was claimed above, the very starting point of our transcendental approach to truth makes it both necessary

---

[51] Van Til, *The Defense of the Faith*, 298.

and inevitable that in the finitude in which we exist there is nowhere else to start. If we do not proceed with a complete epistemological reliance on the revelation that God has made of himself, there is no possibility of truth in knowledge anywhere or at all. From that it follows that we acknowledge, again in admission of our finitude, that we stand at this point before the mystery of God's declaration and revelation.

Our doctrine of mystery is that while mystery may and does exist for man, no mystery exists for God. No embarrassment exists on that account for the Christian thinker whose thought is captive to the Word of God. For we have rejected every notion of human autonomy in relation to the knowledge of God or the things of God. In the finitude in which we bow before our Creator-God, it follows that our knowledge, which is analogical of God's knowledge, while it is true, cannot be comprehensive. We admit the mystery. But in doing so we claim, again by virtue of our creaturehood, finitude, and our rescue from the state of sin, that all of God's revelation, made to us in anthropomorphic terms and forms as it is, necessarily terminates in mystery. Our task as Christian thinkers is to acknowledge that every Christian doctrine terminates in mystery, and that in the light of that two desiderata are imposed on us. First, it is a laziness of thought if we allow our meditations to end before the real locus of mystery has been reached. And secondly, subjecting every thought to the Word of God, our thought is careful not to proceed beyond the point at which the mystery is revealed by God to exist. If we fail in the latter constraint, our theology or philosophy will have proceeded beyond the limits of God's revelation into the forbidden realm of speculation.

Our argument implies a final conclusion. God, we have said, has "according to the counsel of his will foreordained whatsoever comes to pass." That foreordination, we maintain with classic Reformed theology, includes the actions of sentient, decision-making individuals. It includes our right actions and our sin.[52] Embedded within the mystery of God's ordination and providential government is, then, the question with which we began – that of the relation between the ordination of God and the responsible actions of men. We maintain the truth and reality of both halves of that question. God sovereignly works his purposes in the actions of men who are, at the same time, responsible for those acts and the outcomes of them. We acknowledge that there is an established relation of which we do not possess, and in our earthbound finitude are not capable of possessing, an understanding. That is the reality that human action, for which we know are our responsible, is, from the perspective that the eternal, predestinating God commands, compatible with his eternal ordination and determination. We hold, in other words, to what has been referred to as compatibilism, a compatibility between human action and God's ordination. What from our perspective is unconstrained decision and action, uncon-

---

[52] The reality that sinful actions of men are to be brought under the scope of God's eternal ordination has understandably caused difficulty and dispute, and it has led to extensive debate and attempted rebuttal in the literature of open theism already referred to. The Scriptural data in support of the revealed reality, however, are extensive, evidenced, for example, in Genesis 50:20. Joseph there states to his brothers that they intended their action in selling him to the Egyptians "for evil." But "God meant it unto good." Further, God states through the prophet Isaiah, "I form the light, and create darkness. I make peace, and create evil: I the Lord do all these things" (Is. 45:7). The NKJV translation uses the word "calamity" in place of "evil" at that location, as does the ESV. Edward J. Young retains the translation "evil" in his *The Book of Isaiah* (Grand Rapids: Eerdmans, 1972), vol. 3, 194. Young states, "In the very context, then, we are compelled to admit that the word includes all evil, moral as well as calamities," ibid., 200. See Ps. 33:11; Eph. 1:11; and Prov. 21:1-2, "The king's heart is in the hand of the Lord, as the rivers of water: he turneth it whithersoever he will. Every way of man is right in his own eyes: but the Lord pondereth the hearts." Note also the clear statement in Joel 2:25 that while God will restore "the years that the locust hath eaten," the locust, God says, was his "great army which I sent among you."

strained, that is, by external forces, are from God's eternal perspective ordained. We do not hold, as do some forms of contemporary theology such as open theism, to autonomous libertarianism in the sense in which human action is independent of the determining action of the Spirit of God. We hold to the perfection and the fulfillment of God's *decretive* will, though we in our choices and actions may disregard and disobey his *preceptive* will for mankind.

Finally, we bow before the Christ of the Scriptures who came to declare God unto us (John 1:18) and to be our redeemer (Rom. 5:19), and we rest in his gracious word, "If the Son therefore shall make you free, ye shall be free indeed" (John 8:36). That is sufficient to know as to the true freedom of the will and is relevant for time and eternity.

Chapter 5

The Possibility of Redemption

The important contribution to theological doctrine that Anselm made in the eleventh century is contained in his *Cur Deus homo*, "Why God became Man." He explained that in his atonement Christ satisfied the demands of God against sinful man, in that he paid the penalty for the guilt of sin. In the full flower of Reformation theology some four and a half centuries later there was, of course, a richer and more expansive development of doctrine. But even though the church in the years following Anselm's writing was not directly influenced by his achievement, it remains true that his work stands as one of the foundation statements of Christian doctrine.

In this chapter, against the sinful state of the human condition we consider the rescue and relief that God has provided in his Son. In doing so, we adduce the same principle and reach the same conclusion as Anselm. We approach the subject of the satisfaction of Christ by considering firstly, the possibility of redemption as it may be contemplated from the side of God, or as it emanates from the nature and character of

God as he has revealed himself; and secondly, from the side of man the sinner. When the question "Is redemption possible?" is answered in the affirmative it needs to be stated with clarity why that is so. What are the grounds on which the claim is to be advanced not only that redemption is possible, but that God in his mercy has provided a redemption for his people? And what are the grounds on which it is possible to hold a true knowledge of the designs and actions of God that his purpose of redemption implies?

The understanding of the relevant doctrines will be assisted by considering a small number of preliminary issues. First, two alternative ways of conceiving of the divine-human relation will bring to sharper relief the meaning and necessity of the basis from which the discussion of redemption will proceed. The first assumes a metaphysical continuity, or a continuity of being, and consequently a continuity of knowledge, between God and man. It takes up what is referred to as the doctrine of the *analogia entis*, or the analogy of being. The second, which is integral to the Reformed theology, holds, on the contrary, to the Creator-creature distinction. Then after a brief statement regarding the divine decrees the question of the possibility of redemption will be addressed from the sides of both God and man.

Two alternative theological foundations

1. *Metaphysical continuity and the "analogia entis"*

Certain theologies that lie outside the corpus of Reformed belief have maintained that the human person exists in a state of metaphysical continuity with God. God, it is thereby said, does himself exist, and his existence, it is further imagined, is capable of demonstration and proof by the exercise of autonomous and unaided human reason. Man, then, occupies a place in the "chain of being" that emanates from God. That takes up the well-known Roman Catholic dogma of the *analogia entis* on the one hand and Thomas Aquinas' famous "five proofs" for the existence of God on the other. It is not necessary to stay unduly with the scheme of theology in which these presuppositions are embedded.

John Frame has commented as follows regarding the doctrine of *analogia entis* (analogy of being): "The 'analogy of being,' which Aquinas borrowed from Aristotle and Neoplatonism, is a continuum that runs from God at the top to undifferentiated matter at the bottom. God has the most being, bare matter the least. Beings higher on the scale have a greater 'unity between essence and existence,' which means, roughly, that their nature governs their actions and experience."[1] Frame further discusses at some length the respects in which "Van Til criticizes both the Neoplatonic and the Aristotelian elements of Aquinas's theology."[2] Neither do we stay at this point with the so-called "proofs" of God's existence.[3] But for reasons of its implicit denial of the Reformed doctrine, our present interest is in the *analogia entis* assumption.

First, such a starting point, involving as it does the assumption that God, if he exists, exists in metaphysical continuity with man, implies in effect the divinization of man. Man's place in the metaphysically continuous chain of being is, of course, a much lower place. But making any such claim

---

[1] John M. Frame, *Cornelius Van Til: An Analysis of His Thought* (Phillipsburg: P&R, 1995), 90.

[2] Ibid., 258.

[3] The long discussion of the theistic "proofs" in the history of philosophy, taking account in particular of Kant's virtually complete rejection of them and the repeated attempts at their reestablishment that followed, can be examined in many secular philosophy texts. See, for example, the attempted restatement of the ontological proof in R.C. Sproul, John Gerstner, and Arthur Lindsley, *Classical Apologetics: A Rational Defense of the Christian Faith and a Critique of Presuppositional Apologetics*, 93ff, 253ff. A discussion of the "proofs" as they may be reconstructed from the perspectives established by a Reformed presuppositionalist apologetic is contained in Greg L. Bahnsen, *Van Til's Apologetic* (Phillipsburg: P&R Publishing, 1998), 612f.

implies a particular doctrine and belief regarding the establishment of the human person within the universe in which he came to self-consciousness; and that carries with it implications for the assumed competence of human understanding and knowledge. Frame again discusses the "continuum of beings" concept of Neoplatonism and observes with respect to the question of divinization, "The union between God and his emanations amounts to rationalism: the identity of the human mind with the divine. The separation between God and the world implies irrationalism: the ignorance of finite minds, their utter incapacity to know God."[4] Frame comments that "Van Til's analysis of Scholasticism also deals with the 'analogy of being,' which he takes as a kind of Platonic scale of being in which creatures participate by various degrees in divinity."[5] Van Til has observed that "the probative force of [Aquinas'] argument ... depends entirely upon the assumption that the human mind is at least potentially divine."[6]

Those statements are noted at this point because the claims to which they refer distort the biblically-revealed explanation of man as the created image of God. They fatally confuse the image, the derivative and analogical entity that God established, with an imagined participation in the being of God himself.[7] Such a claim forges a linkage between God and man where none has existed or could exist. Taking such a position establishes fatally a continuity that destroys what we shall see as the Creator-creature distinction.[8]

---

[4] Frame, *Cornelius Van Til*, 258.
[5] Ibid., 346.
[6] Van Til, *The Reformed Pastor and Modern Thought* (Philadelphia: Presbyterian and Reformed, 1971), 94.
[7] The use of the words "analogical entity" in this sentence is not to be taken in the sense of the *analogia entis* doctrine, as will be clarified in what follows.
[8] In his *The Reformed Pastor and Modern Thought,* Van Til has discussed the significance of the *analogia entis* theory in Paul Tillich's doctrine of God as the "ground of being" and, as a result, Tillich's

The erroneous assumption of metaphysical continuity, carrying with it a fatal misunderstanding of the being, the person, and the place of man, has implications for doctrinal formulation on several levels. For it implies a corresponding misunderstanding of the significance and the entailment of man's first sin and the entrance of sin to the human condition. What that deviant theology involves is the assumption that all that happened to man as a result of Adam's sin was that he fell to a lower level in the imagined "chain of being." It holds, in effect, that the fall of man involved a metaphysical change, or a change in metaphysical status, and not, as Reformed theology understands it, an ethical lapse. The Roman Catholic theologian, Jacques Maritain, has made the point by observing that "the lack or defect" that was occasioned by the Fall is a defect "in the ontological order."[9]

That defective understanding of the meaning of the Fall follows with firm logic from a defective understanding and doctrine of creation. For the theology that embraces those positions has failed to understand that man as he came from the hands of his Creator was intrinsically and constitutionally holy. His original holiness was not simply a *donum superadditum*, as defective theology often supposes, something added to man after his initial state had been established.[10] That

---

"basic agreement with Roman Catholicism." See Van Til, op. cit, 170 and Tillich, *Systematic Theology* (Chicago: The University of Chicago Press, 1951), Vol.1, *Reason and Revelation, Being and God,* 239-40. Tillich states in that context, "The *analogia entis* gives us our only justification of speaking at all about God."

[9] Maritain, *St. Thomas and the Problem of Evil* (Milwaukee: Marquette University Press, 1942), 6. See Van Til, *The Reformed Pastor and Modern Thought*, 101-104 for further discussion.

[10] The false doctrine that the superadded or "superinduced" gift of righteousness restrained a tendency to disorder in the original constitution of man was argued by Andradius, a member of, and a principal spokesman for, the Roman Catholic Council of Trent. See Archibald Alexander, "Original Sin," in *The Biblical Repertory and Princeton Review,* 1830, reprinted in *Princeton versus the New Divinity* (Edin-

alternative understanding projects its meaning to what was involved in the Fall. From the viewpoint established by the *analogia entis* theory, it follows that when Adam fell he lost the original holiness that had in the first place been added to his initial condition. He was thereby reduced to what he had been before that initial gift of holiness had been given to him.[11] After the Fall our first parent was simply reduced to what, in that respect, he had been initially. He possessed and enjoyed in his new and fallen state the same capacities of faculty with which he had been created. That implies that the rational faculty was not damaged in the respects in which Reformed theology understands the noetic effects, the effects on the mind, of the Fall. Fallen man's epistemic capacity was again what it had initially been. In that manner the virus of Pelagianism is projected to the theology of the church. But if that is taken as an explanation of what was entailed in the Fall, it follows that a further level of significance for the human condition needs to be recognized.

In the same way as God and man share a *being in general*, the theological perspective under review implies that God and man share a *reason in general*. The initial assumption of *metaphysical continuity* is accompanied by a correlative assumption of *epistemological continuity*. That will be seen to throw its light on the possibility of human knowledge and understanding in relation to God's knowledge and his consequent predestinating ordination.

Consider the nature and status of man as he exists after the Fall. We have in view the generality of men in their

---

burgh: Banner of Truth, 2001), 90-114. The doctrine as it came to articulation by the Council of Trent, and as it led to heretical views of the doctrine of original sin, was refuted at that time by Martin Chemnitz (1522-80). The Reformed doctrine of original sin was accorded a full treatment during the same period.

[11] Referring to Aquinas's doctrine Van Til observes that its essence implies that at the Fall man "lost the *donum superadditum*," Van Til, *The Reformed Pastor*, 103.

unregenerate state. The assumption of epistemological continuity stamps the human search for knowledge, along with the processes and criteria of validity that it entails, with a strict rationality. It is thereby assumed that what is knowable to man is knowable completely, given only adequate time and occasion for the knowledge search. The distinction between God's knowledge and man's knowledge is, in those terms and from that perspective, simply and only quantitative. No qualitative, as distinct from quantitative, difference and distinction exists at that point. But that sits oddly with an accompanying assumption that also characterizes unregenerate epistemology. That is the assumption that the universe in which the knowledge process is conducted is a universe of randomness and chance. In it, therefore, anything can happen; and in it, as a result, nothing can be known with certainty. Chance is king, and the laws of probability inform the scope and potential of knowledge discoveries.

The assumption of *epistemological continuity* stamps human investigation as supremely rational, while at the same time the commitment to randomness and chance stamps it as supremely irrational. That brings to focus what has been referred to as the *rationalist-irrationalist dialecticism* of unregenerate thought. In effect, man, at least potentially, knows everything so far as he stands on the rationalist side of the dialectic, or he knows nothing, so far as he capitulates to the irrationalist implications of his assumption of chance.[12]

2. *The Creator-creature distinction*

The alternative viewpoint from which the divine-human relation is contemplated recognizes the reality and the impli-

---

[12] See the comments on "pure rationalism and pure irrationalism" in Van Til, *A Christian Theory of Knowledge* (Philadelphia: Presbyterian and Reformed, 1969), 318.

cations of the *Creator-creature distinction*.[13] Man, as he came from the hands of his Creator, was the analogue of God, the created image of God. When it is said that man is the analogue of God as to his being and his knowledge, it is implied that as such he has *derivative* being, knowledge, and personhood. He is like God in every respect in which a created, finite person can be like his Creator who himself exists in absolute personhood. As the finite analogue of God, man is *like* God but he is not *identical* with God. At no point do we hold to what was referred to earlier as the divinization of man. That means that a *metaphysical discontinuity* exists between God and man. Man, as the image of God, has derivative being, existing in a derivative, analogical, likeness to God as a rational, immortal, spiritual, and speaking person.

That carries with it a corresponding recognition that the *metaphysical discontinuity* between God and man implies also an *epistemological discontinuity*. That means that in the same way as we exist as the derivative analogue of God as to our being, because the infinite God himself exists and is our Creator, so we exist as the derivative analogue of God as to our knowledge and the possibility of knowing. We are the finite analogue of God both as to our being and our knowledge. In short, the fact that absolute being, absolute personhood, and absolute meaning and knowledge exist in God establishes meaning and the discoverability of meaning in the external reality that God has spoken into existence. We can know God and things truly, and there is a true and genuine

---

[13] The Creator-creature distinction is an important motif in Van Til's apologetic theology and may be explored in numerous parts of his work. See his *An Introduction to Systematic Theology* (Philadelphia: Presbyterian and Reformed, 1974), 171, 175. Van Til examines at several points the significance of the Creator-creature distinction for a Christian and a distinctively Reformed philosophy of being (metaphysics) and philosophy of knowledge (epistemology). Necessary conclusions on those levels will inform our discussion in the following text. See also the discussion in Bahnsen, *Van Til's Apologetic*.

correspondence between what God knows and what we know. But there necessarily exist in the mind of God a depth of meaning, and an awareness of relationships between the created entities and histories that he has established and supervises, and a knowledge of the relationships between one point of knowledge and all other points of knowledge, that are inaccessible to us. We can and we do have true knowledge because what we know is an analogue of God's knowledge, but we do not and we cannot have comprehensive knowledge in either a quantitative or qualitative sense.

Unregenerate thought holds to assumptions of both *continuity* and *discontinuity*. It has to be said, also, that both continuity and discontinuity exist in what is to be held as to the meaning of the Christian faith. But vital differences in the content of those assumptions exist in the respective cases. We hold to a *metaphysical* and *epistemological discontinuity* between God and man, established by the reality of the Creator-creature distinction. But we acknowledge also a divinely established *continuity* that will be relevant to the argument that follows. That is the fact that God has established a continuity in all of the eventuation that occurs within created reality, by virtue of his purposive foreordination of "whatsoever comes to pass."[14] What is to be held as the biblically-revealed continuity, the coherence of all intramundane events by virtue of God's predestinating ordination, stands as the polar opposite of the apostate assumption of discontinuity. That latter scheme holds, to the contrary, to the everywhere randomness and chance of history and events. Similarly, the biblically-revealed reality of discontinuity, the Creator-creature distinction, stands as the polar opposite of the apostate assumption of continuity, which posited a continuity of being between God and man.

---

[14] Westminster Shorter Catechism, Question 7.

The divine decrees

The Creator-creature distinction points to the understanding of the human condition and the recognition of the decrees of God on which the possibility of redemption turns. Four aspects of what has been revealed of the divine ordination will provide a basis for the following argument.

First, God's ordination is a triune ordination and his eventuation of what his ordination purposed is a trinitarian eventuation. The covenant of redemption, the agreement between the Persons of the Godhead and the distribution of redemptive offices among them, issued from the deliberations within the predeterminate council of the Godhead before the foundation of the world. The redemptive office of the Father was discharged in the election to eternal life of a determined number of the fallen progeny of Adam, the people he gave to his Son to redeem (John 17:6). The redemptive office of the Son was fulfilled in his coming into the world and taking human nature into union with his divine nature, his providing in that nature a perfect obedience to the law of God as the substitute for his people, and his paying in his death the substitute penalty for their sin. It is the redemptive office of the Holy Spirit to apply to those for whom Christ died the benefits and blessings he purchased for them, to convey to them the blessing of sanctification, and to conduct them to glory.

In all of the works of God external to the Godhead, the so-called *opera ad extra*, all of the three Persons are jointly engaged. Our Lord said, for example, "I speak not of myself; but the Father that dwelleth in me, he doeth the works" (John 14:10). And it was "through the eternal Spirit [Christ] offered himself without spot to God" (Heb. 9:14). But it is clear that it was uniquely the blessed second Person of the Godhead who suffered and died on the sinner's behalf. It was not the Father who suffered in that unique sense. Claims to that effect in the early history of the church, made, for example, by Praxeas and others in the third century and thereby introducing the false teaching of Patripassianism, did not become a part of the church's established belief.[15]

We have spoken of God's "deliberations." But that is to be understood, as all of God's revelation is to be understood, anthropomorphically. God's thoughts are not our thoughts (Is. 55:8), and for that reason we have said that our knowledge is analogical of God's knowledge. A correspondence exists between God's knowledge and our knowledge, but the latter does not coincide with God's knowledge in quality or quantity. God has revealed himself and his purposes to us in terms accommodated to our finite comprehension. His knowledge cannot be said to be sequential, or sequentially deliberative, in the sense in which our thought exists and functions.

Commenting on these and related issues, Van Til observes that "God reveals himself to man according to man's ability to receive his revelation. *All revelation is anthropomorphic.*"[16] In his *The Knowledge of God in Calvin's Theology*, Edward A. Dowey has addressed the anthropomorphic character of God's revelation under the heading of "The Accommodated Character of All Knowledge of God," treating of both "the accommodation of God's revelation to finite comprehension" and "the accommodation to human sinfulness."[17] Calvin comments on Ezekiel 9:3-4, "God cannot be comprehended by us, unless as far as he accommodates himself to our standard. Because therefore God is incomprehensible in himself..."; and on 1 Corinthians 2:7, Calvin comments that "God ... accommodates himself to our capacity in addressing us."

---

[15] See Shedd, *History*, 1:254ff.

[16] Van Til, *A Christian Theory of Knowledge* (Philadelhpia: Presbyterian and Reformed, 1969), 37. See also the extensive discussion in Greg L. Bahnsen, *Van Til's Apologetic*, chap.4.

[17] Edward A. Dowey, op. cit. (Grand Rapids: Eerdmans, 1994), 3ff. See also ibid., 261 for Dowey's "Note on anthropomorphism" and the review of the first edition of Dowey's book by John Murray, reprinted in *Collected Writings of John Murray*, 3:377ff.

Second, all that is involved in God's predestinating ordination and the eventuation of his purpose is for the manifestation of his glory. No higher locus of explanation exists than what is revealed to us as the sovereign will of God. And the dictates of that divine will, moved by "His mere free grace and love,"[18] are directed to the glory of the triune God. God has decreed and done "all to the praise of his glorious grace"[19] (Eph. 1:5-6, 12).

Third, God's sovereign eventuation of what he has purposed is declared extensively in his revealed Word. Not only has he "appointed the elect to glory," but in doing that he has "foreordained the means thereunto."[20] He has done that with the objective not only of conducting his elect to glory, but of providing them in this life with "abundant consolation" because they "sincerely obey the Gospel."[21]

Fourth, as is clearly stated in the same chapter of the confession, in view in God's ordination is the redemption of his people from their inherited sinful state. That is clearly conveyed by the statement that some are "predestinated unto everlasting life," and "others" are "foreordained to everlasting death."[22] The issues of life and death are referable to God's ordination. That the context within which the revelation of God's intention is placed is that of redemption is explicit in the statement that "They who are elected ... are *redeemed* by Christ [and] neither are any other redeemed by Christ."[23] The triune work of the Godhead is contemplated, first, in the fact that God has "freely and unchangeably ordain(ed) whatsoever comes to pass" in that connection; second, in the fact that "they who are elected, being fallen in Adam, are redeemed by Christ"; and third, in the promise that those who "are effec-

---

[18] Westminster Confession of Faith, III, V.
[19] Idem.
[20] Ibid., III, VI.
[21] Ibid., III, VIII.
[22] Ibid., III, III.
[23] Ibid., III, VI.

tually called unto faith in Christ by His Spirit ... are kept by His power, through faith, unto salvation."[24]

The possibility of redemption that we now address brings into focus two issues: first, that of the promise of redemption itself; and second, what we contemplate as the possibility of it. The latter of those issues is our immediate concern. We begin with the question of possibility. After we have addressed the question of the *possibility* of redemption, we shall change our perspective and speak of the possibility of *redemption*. In the first of those questions the matter of redemption is regarded from the perspective of what is revealed regarding God in his being, knowledge, and ordination. The latter question is addressed from the perspective of our own awareness, knowledge, and inquiry.

The *possibility* of redemption

Was it necessary, it might be asked, that God should set forth a plan of redemption? The divine decretive decision and the plan of redemption did, it has been seen, emanate from the predeterminate council of the Godhead. That outcome is stated clearly and repeatedly in the pages of the Scriptures (Eph. 1:4, 1 Peter 1:2, Acts 2:23, 4:28). But in the divine deliberations and ordinations no necessity attached to that outcome that is available to our inspection beyond the free will of God as that was informed by his eternal love. There could not have been any law or requirement external to and beyond God, to which it was necessary for him to subscribe. If the latter had been the case, then the God about whom we would be speaking would not be the sovereign God who has revealed himself in the Scriptures.

The decree of God to redeem, however, has been revealed and is clearly before us. That fact directs us to the meaning of the "possibility" of the decree of redemption in

---

[24] Ibid., III, passim.

the sense in which it is now intended. It points to our understanding of what the reality of the decree involves. We look, then, at the possibility of God's ordination and what has been revealed as the nature of it.

At this point we recall our previous discussion of the epistemological discontinuity between God and man. We hold to what we have already adduced as the Creator-creature distinction. That earlier argument is now expanded by stating that there does not exist a *univocal* relation between God's knowledge and speech on the one hand and our knowledge and speech on the other. There does not exist on that level a *univocal* relation (meaning that in that case there would be an exact equivalence between what God knows and says and what we know and say), nor is the relation in view *equivocal* (meaning that there would then be no correspondence at all between those two levels of knowing and speaking). The relation to be contemplated is that of *analogy*. The God-man relation in knowledge and speech is, to summarize, neither univocal nor equivocal, but is analogical. We know different things at different times, and what we know we know by a process of sequential discovery. But in God, who created time, there is no such succession of moments. There is no succession of moments in either the being or the knowledge of God. God did not have to wait to discover anything about himself. God knew himself completely in one eternal act of knowing.[25] And, as our recognition of the anthropomorphism of revelation has alerted us to recall, there is not, and there could not have been, any succession of moments in the knowledge of God. In his one eternal act of knowing God knew all things regarding external reality and its ordained history. God knew all of the facts of created reality because he thought those facts, established all of the potential of their identity, and set them in their temporally unfolding histories before the foundation of the world.

---

[25] See Van Til, *The Defense of the Faith*, 37.

Those conclusions are relevant to the divine decrees and foreordination of human events and, in particular, to the decree to redeem. That relevance is contained in the fact that those divine decrees are what they are, and they have the salvific significance attached to them, because they are integral to that one eternal act of knowing which constitutes the knowledge of God. Why and how, then, do we answer the question as to the *possibility* of redemption, or, in the present context, the possibility of the decree to redeem? What is to be said as to *why there should ever have been any possibility of redemption*? We answer that the very awareness of the being of God, as he has disclosed himself in his timeless and eternal character, requires us to see that the divine decree is, in fact, integral to the very disclosure of the nature of the being of God himself. In short, as we shall now go on to see, the God who has revealed himself to us is a *decreeing* God.

The conclusion of the matter is that *it is not possible for us in our finitude to contemplate God in his eternal being as distinct and separable from what it is he has revealed himself to have thought and done*. God is not to us an abstract entity. Our theology must rise beyond the levels of abstraction, such as that to which the earlier Greeks, for example, were committed, to the level of the concrete. God has not revealed himself to us as an abstract entity to whom we are called upon to add, if we are to know him, certain characteristics of being or descriptions of thought and action. On the contrary, what God has revealed as to his attributes, actions, purposes, ordinations, and works is integral to his disclosure of himself as he exists. We do not first acknowledge God as existing in an unattributed form to which we add certain descriptive attributes. We acknowledge that God has revealed himself as the one true, living, and only God who is, by the very description that he has given of himself, the decreeing God. We do not and cannot separate the disclosure of God as to his being from his disclosure of his attributes and decretive actions. *The God we know is a decreeing God.* Van Til wrote, "The attributes of God are not characteristics that God has developed gradually; they are fundamental to his being."[26] What is here said of the *attributes* of God is to be said also of the knowledge, purposes, and ordinations of God, as he exists in what is for us the incomprehensible timelessness of his being.

That can be put differently by saying that we do not and cannot draw a conceptual distinction between the *essence* of God and the *attributes* and *actions* of God. Or to put it differently, we do not have direct access to knowledge of the essence of God. Rather, the essence of God is disclosed to us in the revelation of his attributes and actions. The essence of God is not to be understood as distributed among his attributes, but is to be seen as fully contained in each of what we have come to understand as his attributes. Calvin comments, "What is God? Men who pose this question are merely toying with idle speculations. It is more important for us to know of what sort he is and what is consistent with his nature."[27] Calvin states further that "the most perfect way of seeking God ... is not for us to attempt with bold curiosity to penetrate to the investigation of his essence ... but for us to contemplate him in his works whereby he ... communicates himself."[28] As to the knowability of God, Berkhof states, "Reformed theology holds that God can be known, but that it is impossible for man to have a knowledge of Him that is exhaustive."[29] He continues, "Luther distinguishes between the *Deus absconditus* (hidden God) and the *Deus revelatus* (revealed God) [meaning] that even in His revelation God has not manifested Himself entirely *as He is essentially*, but as to His essence still remains shrouded in impenetrable darkness. We know God only in so far as He enters into relations with us. Calvin

---

[26] Van Til, *The Defense of the* Faith, 10.
[27] Calvin, *Institutes,* I, ii, 2.
[28] Ibid., I, v, 9.
[29] Berkhof, *Systematic Theology*, 30.

too speaks of the Divine essence as incomprehensible."[30] As Turretin comments, "The divine attributes are the essential properties by which he [God] makes himself known to us."[31]

The foregoing means that the "possibility" of redemption is inherent in the very being of God who has disclosed himself to us as the decreeing, gracious, redeeming God. The God we know, we have said, is a decreeing God. There is no other God. We therefore bow before the only, wise, and decreeing God in adoration and worship. Redemption is "possible," then, for reasons that are lost to our full understanding in the wise and perfect and gracious will of God. Of God's own eternal and timeless knowledge of his will we have only a finite and analogical understanding.

That conclusion may be thrown into further relief by drawing attention to the meaning of possibility itself as a category of knowing. In our ordinary processes of knowing we speak of the possibility of this or that, or of the probability of this or that occurrence. But what is now at issue is the fact that the meaning of "possibility" requires the acknowledgement that *only that is "possible," in the history of human affairs, which God has already ordained and established by his eternal decree*. That returns us to the statement that God is a *decreeing* God. But there does not exist any category of possibility to which God was, or could have been, subject. That is the same thing as saying that there does not exist, and there could not have existed, any law or category of meaning to which God was subject in defining himself or forming his decrees. Van Til argues similarly that "Either one presupposes God back of the ideas of possibility or one presupposes that the idea of possibility is back of God. Either one says with historic Reformed theology on the basis of Scripture that what God determines and only what God determines is possible, or one says with all non-Christian forms of thought that possibil-

---

[30] Ibid., italics in original.
[31] Turretin, *Elenctic Theology*, 1:187.

ity surrounds God."[32] All that is and exists, and all of the histories of all that exists, are what they are because of the sovereign, decreeing will of God.

Our argument thus far has turned on three essential points. First, the decrees of God are the decrees of the only, true, living, and sovereign God, who has revealed himself as a gracious decreeing God. Second, the decrees of God are in themselves intrinsic to what is revealed to us as to the being of God. We know no other God than the all-wise decreeing God. Third, our epistemic grasp of the meaning, necessity, and possibility of those decrees is what it is by virtue of our boundedness in time and the necessity, within that boundedness, of contemplating the decrees and actions of God who exists and decrees outside of the time that he created. The manner of our knowing, and the qualitative extent of it, are different from that of God.

At this point, we turn to address not only the *possibility* of redemption and the redemptive decree, as we have seen that to be inherent in the very Godness of God as he has revealed himself. Coming clearly into view also is the redemption that was thus possible by virtue of the nature and the will of God from whose counsel the decree issued.

The possibility of *redemption*

By the eternal decree to redeem, "some men and angels are predestinated unto everlasting life; and others are foreordained to everlasting death."[33] In the case of the men who are the subjects of that decree, their rescue from the state of sin into which they had fallen is at issue. Our objective is to consider the bearing on that of the relations we have brought to focus in the preceding sections. We are concerned again, now from a different perspective and vantage point, with the

---

[32] Van Til, *The Defense of the Faith*, 345-46.
[33] Westminster Confession of Faith, III, III.

nature of the human knowledge potential and its relation to the knowledge of God. Our immediate concern is with the reasons why our own rational commitment to the doctrine of the divine redemptive decree is necessary.

If, again, our thought is directed by the reality of the Creator-creature distinction, two things are to be said. First, given what has been referred to as the *epistemological discontinuity* between God and man that is implied by that distinction, and given that our understanding and knowledge is *analogical* of God's understanding and knowledge, it follows that *there is a residual sense in which we cannot "understand" the divine decree to which we are now referring*. We are not saying that we do not have a true awareness of the effectiveness of the decree as to our salvation, of the intention and scope of it, and of the promise of eternal felicity it conveys. But because the decree itself is inherent in the mind of God, we possess only an *analogical*, but true, replica, and not an identical and *univocal* reproduction of it. For that reason the meaning of the decree, in its full eternal import, is beyond our epistemic grasp. We are reminding ourselves that God is in heaven and we are on earth.

Second, we ask why, from the perspective of human knowledge, it is necessary for us to bow before the declaration of God's decreed purpose. The curtain of mystery in which the eternal divine decree has been established has been lifted for us to a degree. We know that the only, true, living, and eternally gracious God has told us clearly something of his purpose. He has given us a partial revelation of his purpose, and in his Word he has preserved to us a partial record of the partial revelation that he has made to men. But there is still more to be known. We begin to grasp something of what the apostle conceived when he said there has not "entered into the heart of man, the things which God hath prepared for them that love him" (1 Cor. 2:9). But what, we ask, establishes the necessity of our consent and commitment to the revelation of the divine decree of redemption that we now have before us?

The question strikes to the heart of the difficulty that many have, even many among truly regenerate, believing children of God, with the doctrine of God's eternal election. What, then, in the light of the level of understanding that God has conveyed to us, should dispel the difficulty that arises at this point? The answer is twofold. First, it is necessary for us to see that there is no other way, no method or procedure other than that established in the eternal divine decree, by which redemption from the entailment of sin could have been accomplished. But why is that so? The answer follows that if, by the grace of the Spirit of God, we grasp a true understanding of the state of sin into which we were cast by Adam's fall, as well as the resulting extent of our inability to do anything to save ourselves from the entailment of that sin, then we also see that it is absolutely necessary that God alone can and must save us. That he has done so is eloquently proclaimed in this very doctrine of his gracious, eternal election. In short, the doctrine of election will command assent only when the doctrine of sin commands assent. A defective doctrine of sin will lead only to a fragmented awareness of God's eternal purpose and will inhibit one's consent to what God in his gospel has declared. At the root of the difficulty to concur with the doctrine of God's election is a defective doctrine of sin, and with it a defective doctrine of the sovereign and gracious love of God for the sinners he has called to himself in Christ.

That leads to the second answer to why difficulty inheres in one's possible response to this gracious revelation of God's election. To put it starkly, the problem is that man in sin is so frequently ready to assume to himself an autonomy and a capacity for understanding and decision that he does not possess. That takes us back to our starting point in this discussion. It means that the individual person too readily assumes to himself or herself that the capacities of the faculties of soul were not damaged and cursed with the disabilities that are inherent in the bequest of Adam's fall. We are, as we said at the beginning, too readily little Pelagians. We don't readily acknowledge the noetic effects of the Fall. We are reluctant to assent to the fact that "the natural man receiveth not the things of the Spirit of God; for they are foolishness unto him; neither can he know them, because they are spiritually discerned" (1 Cor. 2:14). Our difficulties arise because we too often make the same mistake as that by which Adam dragged us down into sin. We assume to ourselves an autonomy that we do not possess. It was the false assertion of autonomy that constituted our first parents' sin.

Why, then, is assent to this doctrine of God's eternal election necessary? Assent is necessary, first, because as a result of our depravity and lost condition in the state of sin, there was no other way in which we could be redeemed and come to the prospect of eternal felicity. And assent is necessary, secondly, because in our existence in this world we are, as has been argued, the derivative analogue of God who created us in his image, and we are altogether dependent upon him. That is true, both as to our being and all of our awareness and understanding.

But this high subject of the decretive will of God cannot be left without a final statement and warning. At issue is God's double decree whereby some "are predestinated unto everlasting life; and others foreordained to everlasting death."[34] The questions arise, though not all of their implications and scope can be traced at this late stage, of how a true and life-forming grasp of the revelation at this point is to be gained, and to whom, by the grace of God, such an apprehension is conveyed. Only one final comment, by way of implication of what has already been said, will be made.

We are not speaking in this context of a result of thought that is available to autonomous and unenlightened human reason. The address of unregenerate reason to the revelation of the decretive will of God leads only to a blank and dark-

---

[34] Westminster Confession of Faith, III, III.

ened fatalism and an agnostic determinism. To the contrary, antecedent to a true understanding on these levels is the regenerating illumination of the Spirit of God that bequeaths saving faith in Christ. Objectively, the work of Christ as the material cause of our redemption, and subjectively, our vision of all of God's grace communicated in him, provide the only efficient complex in which the doctrine of God's electing purpose is to be viewed. In Christ alone, in his perfect sacrifice for sinners, do we find the refuge of faith.

Let us hold to the doctrine of the fallen and sinful state to which we were reduced in Adam, to the gratuitous love of God that moved his electing will, to the substitutionary and meritorious work of Christ that dealt with our liability and guilt, and to the sovereign applicatory work of the Holy Spirit. Then the conclusion of the Psalmist will burn itself into our consciousness with life-determining significance, "With thee is the fountain of life; *in thy light shall we see light*" (Ps. 36:9). God grant that it may be so.

Chapter 6

The Cosmic Significance of Christ

Divine redemption has addressed the human condition. Its premise rests in the will of God that was influenced by his love for his people. Its process required the coming into the world of the eternal Son, from the glory that he had with the Father before creation and the beginning of time. He came as Jesus Christ to save his people from their sins. The mystery of his incarnation, his suffering in his human nature, his substitutionary death and his resurrection and ascension to his heavenly session, have called forth the wonder and the worship of those who believe in him. Through the ages it has challenged the antagonism of his detractors. But the redemptive Christ-event stands as the watershed of all human history. The appearance of Jesus Christ has challenged all that the history of thought has interpreted as meaningful in the human journey. Through the ages prior to his incarnation and in the two millennia since, the promise of his coming and his prominence in the determination of history have called loudly for explanation. And yet the dual mystery of his entrance to the world remains. Who is Jesus Christ? And what is the significance of his coming and of the work that he came to do?

The answers that have been given have not been uniform in their import and doctrinal relevance. They have not projected a consistent testimony of the church. The defense of the deity of Christ, for which Athanasius contended against the heresies that troubled the Christian confession so long ago, has not carried universal or consistent conviction. It is remarkable that in the name of a Christian apology in our time the heresy again clamors for recognition that Jesus Christ was a person less than the eternal Son of God. But the apostolic witness is to the contrary. When the apostle observed that "great is the mystery of godliness," he at the same time insisted that in the person of Jesus Christ "God was manifested in the flesh" (1 Tim. 3:16); and he had earlier maintained that Jesus Christ was "God blessed for ever," or as another translation has it, he was "the eternally blessed God" (Rom. 9:5). At the same point of his letter to Timothy, Paul stated that Christ is "over all." That comprehensive and all-determining rule and authority points to what we have now referred to as the cosmic significance of Christ. That cosmic significance turns on his fulfillment of the messianic-redemptive assignment he undertook in the council of the Godhead before the foundation of the world.

The apostle John underlined the Pauline emphasis. He set forth in his first epistle the touchstone of true Christian confession. "Believe not every spirit," he said, "but try the spirits whether they are of God." And the test of legitimacy follows: "Every spirit that confesseth that Jesus Christ is come in the flesh is of God" (1 John 4:1-2). Christ not only came as the Messiah who had been promised from the beginning, from the very time of our first parents' lapse (Gen. 3:15), but he came from a pre-existence with the Father and the Holy Spirit. Christ came, John stated in his gospel record, as "the only begotten Son which is in the bosom of the Father [and] he hath declared him [unto us]" (John 1:18).

In asking, "Who is Jesus Christ?" we do not recall in detail at this point the early controversies that troubled the church. The heresies of docetic Gnosticism and the subsequent Arianism and Sabellianism have already been noted. The docetics had claimed that only a phantom body appeared in the man Jesus Christ.[1] Gnosticism had argued on several grounds, related mainly to its insistence on a distinction between the material and the spiritual worlds, between the evil and the good, that God could not have assumed human flesh and a human nature.[2] The Arians had argued that Christ was a creature of God and was therefore less than divine. Sabellianism, a form of modalism that anticipated latter-day Unitarianism, claimed that what Christianity worshipped as the Second and Third Persons of the Godhead were only different manifestations or emanations of the one God.

Important for the present is the outcome of the so-called Christological settlement of those earlier years. Jesus Christ was eternally God; he was fully God in human nature. When he walked the dusty roads of Galilee and Judea, when he healed the sick, gave sight to the blind and raised the dead, he was, as to both his divine and his human natures, in this world; but as to his divine nature he was with the Father and the Holy Spirit in heaven as well. Mystery of mysteries, our Lord himself stated that the One who spoke with Nicodemus in that nocturnal encounter was "the Son of man which is in heaven" (John 3:13).[3] Jesus Christ, as to his divine nature, possessed all of the glory and attributes of the Godhead; the full essence of the Godhead resides in him (Col. 2:9).

---

[1] On docetism see Cunningham, *Historical Theology,* 1:124; Bengt Hägglund, *History of Theology,* trans. Gene J. Lund (St. Louis: Concordia Publishing House, 1968), 21.

[2] On Gnosticism see Cunningham, op. cit., 125; Hägglund, op. cit., 33ff.

[3] A discussion of the statement, "Who is in heaven," is contained in William Hendriksen, *Exposition of the Gospel According to John* (Grand Rapids: Baker, 2 Vols., 1953-54), 2:500-501.

The Cosmic Significance of Christ

It will anticipate an important conclusion to observe a significant implication of that reality. In his divine nature, Jesus Christ retained the incommunicable attribute of omnipresence. Now that he sits at "the right hand of the Majesty on high" (Heb. 1:3), that attribute continues to come to expression in the divine immanence in the world and in the execution of God's works of providence. On the night he was betrayed our Lord shared with his disciples the supper discourses that are spread over the thirteenth to the seventeenth chapters of John's gospel. On that occasion he gave the promise to his disciples, and through them to those for whom he was about to die: "I will not leave you comfortless; I will come to you" (John 14:18; compare John 17:20). That promise was fulfilled in a unique sense in the coming of the Holy Spirit of Christ on the day of Pentecost. But in it is to be seen the reality that Christ in his divine Person has come to be with his people. The Christian walks in this world in the company of his Lord. There is not an inch of space, as there is not an instant of time, in which the full essence of the Godhead is not immanent. But beyond that reality, the presence of God in human affairs comes to specific expression in the lives of his people. Christ, by the Spirit whom he has sent, walks with them in their journey in this world.

Jonathan Edwards, eighteenth-century theologian and preacher, reached a related conclusion in his essay on "The End for Which God Created the World." That end or purpose Edwards capsules in the statement that "a disposition in God, as an original property of his nature, to an emanation of his own infinite fullness, was what excited him to create the world; and so, that the emanation itself was aimed at by him as a last end of the creation."[4] There is beyond doubt both insight and truth in Edwards' conclusion. But we may refer in

---

[4] Jonathan Edwards, op. cit., quoted in John Piper, *God's Passion for His Glory: Living the Vision of Jonathan Edwards* (Wheaton, Ill.: Crossway Books, 1998), 151.

more precise terms to the purpose in God's creation and in all of his providential intervention in the world. It was God the Father's design and objective that in all things the Son might be glorified. That objective of the glorification of his Son throws its light on the cosmic significance of Jesus Christ, his Person and his work. In his High Priestly prayer our Lord prayed, "Father ... glorify thy Son.... Father, glorify thou me with thine own self with the glory which I had with thee before the world was" (John 17:1, 5). God is glorified in the emanation of his perfections and in the salvation of those whom he gave to his Son to redeem; and the Son is glorified in the fulfillment of his messianic assignment and in his elevation to the position of rule and authority at the right hand of the Father. The writer to the Hebrews has explained that Christ has been appointed "Heir of all things" (Heb. 1:2).

The dual mystery of Christ

When we ask, "Who was Jesus Christ?" two questions come into view. First, what is to be said on the basis of God's revelation in his Word of Christ's eternal status within the Godhead, in which status he participated in the intratrinitarian communication that established the purpose and covenant of redemption? And second, what, in the light of that, was the redemptive office and assignment he undertook and the covenantal commitment he made to the Father and the Holy Spirit? The first of those questions has been addressed briefly in what has been said of Christ's identity in his taking our human nature, yet without sin, into union with his divine nature. The second question points to the nature of his redemptive accomplishment. It alerts us to the dual mystery of Christ: first, the mystery of his divine Personhood; and second, the mystery of his entrance into the time that he had created. No more compelling mystery can engage the mind than that God who exists in timeless eternity entered into the real historical sequence of time that he established.

The very notion and the revealed reality of timeless eternity challenges the reflective mind. But the question, "Who was Jesus Christ?" forces the realization that God the Father generated the Son in his eternal timeless day. That is mystery to us. God has not in any sense lifted the veil for us at that point. Augustine wrestled with the question of the meaning of time and of the generation of God the Son in the eternal day outside of time. "Your 'years' are 'one day' (Ps. 89:4; 2 Peter 3:8), and your 'day' is not any and every day but Today, because your Today does not yield to a tomorrow, nor did it follow on a yesterday. Your Today is eternity. So you begat one coeternal with you, to whom you said: 'Today I have begotten you' (Ps. 2:7; Heb. 5:5). You created all times and you existed before all times. Nor was there any time when you did not exist. There was therefore no time when you had not made something, because you made time itself."[5]

Augustine is there saying that God the Son was begotten in the eternal Today. The eternal generation of the Son, and more extensively what is to be referred to as the *opera ad intra*, the works of the Godhead internal to the Godhead, are to be acknowledged as outside of time. Our grasp of what is revealed to us slips if the eternal generation of the Son is contemplated as a sequential generation in time. We cannot ascribe a temporal dimension or a sequential process to it. We are bounded in time, as to our being, our knowledge, our epistemic capacities, and our ability to think rightly; we cannot, therefore, have any conception of what God in his triune being has done in and with himself in establishing himself in triune form. We simply do not know. We cannot know. We either accept the mystery of his revelation and bow before him in worship, or we reject what he has clearly declared of himself and allow our timebound logic to force us to a position of agnosticism.

---

[5] Augustine, *Confessions*, trans. Henry Chadwick (Oxford: Oxford University Press, 1991), 230.

God has revealed himself as eternally existing as a trinity in unity. But in our reference at an earlier point to the defense of the autotheotic nature of Christ that Athanasius entered against the Arians, our focus was on the eternal self-existence of God the Son who became Jesus Christ for our redemption. The Christological settlement at the Council of Chalcedon gave doctrinal expression to that fact. When the question of the self-existence of the Son of God is raised there may well be a tendency to contemplate God as he has revealed himself as a trinity of Persons and to focus our thought, as a result, on the self-existence of each of the Persons separately considered. But that is the pressure of our timebound logic that we must avoid. On the contrary, in asking the question our thought falls on the revealed fact of the *unity* of the Godhead. Augustine has alerted us to the reality that each of the Persons of the Godhead is characterized by self-existence because the unity of God, or God in his oneness, is characterized by self-existence.

The God we know, the God who has revealed himself, is not known except as he is known as both one and three. In our thought about God the threeness does not take precedence over the oneness, nor the oneness take precedence over the threeness. When we think of our Savior we think of him as fully God, with all that is meant and implied by all that is revealed regarding the attributes of God. Our timebound logic should not be allowed to suggest that we can contemplate any one of the three Persons, the Father, the Son, or the Holy Spirit, apart from his full essential existence in the one. Each of the Persons is characterized by self-existence because each is fully God, and the full essence of the Godhead resides in each of the Persons, but the mystery of that reality has not been revealed to us. William Cunningham, distinguished Scottish theologian of the mid-nineteenth-century, has observed, "The eternal generation of the Son, then, just means the communication from eternity, *in some ineffable and mysterious way*, of the divine nature and essence."[6] Cunningham has referred to those who "deny or reject the doctrine of Christ's eternal Sonship" as falling subject to "the fallacy of the argument [that] proceeds upon the assumption that generation, – and what it involves or implies when applied to the divine nature, – must be the same as when applied to men, and that the same or an analogous inference may be deduced from it in both cases."[7]

The works of God internal to the Godhead, that were referred to as the *opera ad intra*, are to be understood as the eternal generation of the Son and the procession of the Holy Spirit from the Father and the Son. But beyond the mystery of the *opera ad intra* there is also the mystery of what God has done for our redemption. That refers to the works of God external to the Godhead, the *opera ad extra*. God established within himself a distribution of redemptive offices. On that our salvation turns. The mystery of godliness extends to the very incarnation of the Son and his assumption of sinless human nature. It expands to the fact of his existence in this world in both his divine and human natures at the same time as he was in his divine nature with the Father (John 3:13). And it involves his retention in his Personhood in this world of all the attributes of deity that were eternally and fully his. It encompasses his setting aside the insignia of his glory but not setting aside the glory that he retained in his full divine being.

That very fact directs us to the redemptive office and assignment that Christ undertook in his discharge of his eternal covenantal commitment. The redemption that Christ provided in his life and death, in his active and passive obedience, is explicable by reason that it was a real work of substitution effected in real historical time. The question has frequently troubled the church as to who it was for whom Christ died. For whom was he the substitute sin-bearer? He has himself

---

[6] Cunningham, *Historical Theology*, 1:301, italics added.
[7] Ibid., 299.

answered that question eloquently in his High Priestly prayer. He died a death for the people whom God the Father had given him to redeem. "I have manifested thy name unto the men which thou gavest me out of the world," he prayed, "thine they were, and thou gavest them me" (John 17:6). He continues, "I pray not for the world, but for them which thou hast given me.... Neither pray I for these alone, but for them also which shall believe on me through their word" (John 17:9, 20). Here our Lord articulated in certain terms the particularity of the redemption he provided. It was a redemption for God's people, for those whom God had chosen in his Son before the foundation of the world (Eph. 1:4).

Consider again our Lord's magnificent discourse on his identity as the good shepherd, recorded in John 10. "The good shepherd," he said, "giveth his life for the sheep" (John 10:11). And the "sheep" to whom he referred, he said, he knew "by name" (John 10:3). The Jews, however, demurred. "Many of them said, He hath a devil, and is mad" (John 10:20). Against their expostulation and repudiation of his claim, Christ made a definitive statement as to the particularity of his redemption, "But ye believe not, because ye are not of my sheep" (John 10:26). The answer to the question of the extent of the atonement, as that has occupied the Reformed theological mind, is the consistent testimony of the Scriptures. We hold to the revealed reality of a particular atonement. Christ died for particular people.

Let us ask the question in a different form. To ask, "For whom did Christ die?" is to ask who it was whose sin was imputed to Christ in his death. A reciprocal imputation was involved in the death of Christ. The guilt of the sin of the people for whom he died was imputed to Christ. In the redemptive action of the Father, Christ was by that imputation constituted guilty. He was guilty not of any sin of his own, because he was the sinless and impeccable Son of God. But he was *constituted* guilty of the sin of those for whom he was the redemptive substitute, in order that God could *declare* him guilty. God then laid on him a substitute punishment that expunged the liability to his wrath that the sin of his people warranted. The punishment for sin that he bore was a substitute penalty in both extent and time. For the full wrath of God in infinite extent was there addressed to the Son. But that wrath was not borne to eternity. On the cross the sin-bearing was complete, and on the third day Christ rose again, conqueror over death and the grave. In that, he introduced his redeemed people to the prospect of eternal inheritance with him (Heb. 9:15). In that action the reciprocity of imputation existed in the fact that the righteousness of Christ was imputed to, or placed to the account of, those who were the subjects of his atonement. They were thereby *constituted* righteous by that imputation of forensic righteousness in order that God could *declare* them righteous. Thus God, who cannot lie and cannot act unjustly, was "just, and the justifier of him which believeth in Jesus" (Rom. 3:26).

In that transaction of double imputation God set his love on people who were the objects of his wrath. John speaks of God's love and his wrath when he says, "Herein is love, not that we loved God, but that he loved us, and sent his Son to be the propitiation for our sins" (1 John 4:10; compare 1 John 2:2, Rom. 3:25, Heb. 2:17). By reason of Christ's substitutionary sin-bearing God is now at peace with his people. "We have peace with God" (Rom. 5:1). "There is therefore now no condemnation to them which are in Christ Jesus" (Rom. 8:1). In the substitutionary work of Christ the love of God is set forth, and in that alone do we find the refuge of faith.

It has been widely claimed, however, that the atonement Christ provided was a general or universal atonement. By that is meant that Christ paid the penalty for the sins of everyone, of all individuals. The question as to whether an individual is saved, in the sense that his or her entitlement to heaven is established, turns, in that scheme of things, on whether that person does or does not accept the benefit of the atonement that Christ provided. Every person is thus imagined to possess a sovereign authority and capacity for decision in that ultimate sense. The disabling virus of human autonomy exerts its damning impulse at that point. It is clear that not all are saved. God the Holy Spirit conducts to glory only those who come to Christ in repentance and faith. Consider that more ultimate reality in the following terms.

If, as in the foregoing argument, it were assumed that Christ provided a general atonement in the sense stated, then having regard to the fact that not all are saved, a wedge would be driven between the work of the Son in his atonement and the work of the Holy Spirit. For it is the work of the Spirit to call men to faith. That wedge would exist because some individuals for whom Christ died, and for whom he thereby paid the penalty for the sin that disabled their entry to heaven, would nevertheless be left to the eternal perdition their sin warranted. A wedge would also be driven between the work of the Son and the work of the Father. For the Father, the Word of God has clearly revealed, designed the salvation of a definitively stated number of people. True it is that God's promise to Abraham was that his seed would be as numberless as the sand of the seashore and as the stars of the heavens (Gen. 15:5; 22:17). And as Paul stated to the Galatian church, those whom the Holy Spirit has conducted to Christ are the seed of Abraham (Gal. 3:29). But it is also true that Christ gave his life for the "sheep," the people whom God the Father gave to him for that purpose. Errant doctrine thus drives a wedge between the works of the Father, the Son, and the Holy Spirit.

It follows that if a wedge is thus driven between the *works* of the Persons of the Godhead, a wedge is thereby driven between the *knowledge* of the Persons of the Godhead. And further, if, as the damaging supposition implies, a wedge is driven between the *knowledge* of the Persons, a wedge is thereby driven between the *being* of the Father, the Son, and the Holy Spirit. By that fact, then, the revealed doctrine of the simplicity and singularity of the Godhead is destroyed. On the contrary, the full essence of the Godhead, the being and the knowledge, resides fully in each of the Persons, the Father, the Son, and the Holy Spirit. It is necessary for that reason to hold to the particularity of the atonement.[8]

Our immediate concern is to bring into focus the implication of what has now been said for its bearing on the cosmic significance of Christ. In the light of the trinity in unity in which God exists, we recognize the reality that an *intratrinitarian communication* occurred in timeless eternity between the Persons of the Godhead. That intratrinitarian communication is here referred to as the first of the dual mysteries of Christ. It lies at the heart of what is to be said regarding the cosmic significance of Christ. The terms of what was to be involved in that were communicated by the Father to the Son before the beginning of time.

We have spoken of two aspects of the mystery of Christ. The second again falls with unique focus on the cosmic significance of the work of Christ. It is that Christ's redemptive work was effected in real historical time.[9] Time, as Van Til, following Augustine, has stated it, "is God-created as a mode of finite existence."[10] It is relevant to our present argument to consider Van Til's comment on the position taken by the nineteenth-century Arminian theologian, Richard

---

[8] The erroneous argument regarding the extent of the atonement has been answered definitively in John Owen's *The Death of Death in the Death of Christ* (see chap. 1 above). Following the Reformation and the consolidation of Reformed doctrine in the Canons of Dordt, a mediating theology arose under the name of Amyraldianism. That substantially defective body of doctrine was given a revival in R. T. Kendall, *Calvin and English Calvinism to 1649* (Oxford: Oxford University Press, 1979) and was replied to effectively by Paul Helm, *Calvin and the Calvinists* (Edinburgh: Banner of Truth, 1982).

[9] The question of time has been discussed more fully in Vickers, *The Fracture of Faith*, chap. 4, "God in Eternity and Time." Reference to the expansive literature on the subject can be examined there, notably the work of Augustine, Helm, Dabney, Reymond, and Van Til.

[10] Van Til, *An Introduction to Systematic Theology*, 66.

Watson, in his *Theological Institutes* "with respect to the knowledge that God has of temporal events." Van Til observes, "If we introduce time or succession of moments into the consciousness of God in order that we may understand how God is related to time we have to ask ourselves in turn how the consciousness of God is related to the being of God. Thus we should have to introduce succession of moments into the being of God."[11] The revealed doctrine of the timelessness of God would thereby be destroyed.

One further preliminary observation is in order before the cosmic significance of Christ is addressed more directly. It is that because Christ has assumed our human nature to himself he has not, and he will not, divest himself of it. That means that we in our finitude, a finitude that will not be transcended even in the eternal glory to which we are destined, will necessarily experience that glory in an eternally unending passage of time. That is so, though the precise nature of the eternal occurrences in time are, in our present timebound consciousness, beyond our grasp. But our Lord's submission of himself in his human nature to the sequences of time evinces the profound extent to which he has identified himself with us in order to secure our redemption.

The cosmic significance of Christ

The redemptive work of Christ has cosmic significance because of both the meaning of his messianic assignment and the perfection with which its obligations were discharged. His life and death had precise salvific significance. In his death he definitively saved his people. In his death he provided a penal sacrifice for sin, in that he paid the penalty that was due by reason of the wrath of God against sin. But a wider and more comprehensive significance attaches to the redemptive work of Christ. The accomplishment of that work is too narrowly

---

[11] Van Til, *The Defense of the Faith*, 35-36.

specified and is seriously diminished in its import if attention is paid only to its specific salvific effect. It is true that the Scriptures explain expansively that in his death Christ paid the penalty for the sins of his people. He confirmed their title to heaven by his perfect keeping of the law of God in his active obedience. He fulfilled for those who had been committed to him by the Father their previously unfulfilled obligations under the covenant of works that Adam had repudiated.[12] But the significance of the Person and work of Christ has a wider and more comprehensive denotation. In his death he cleansed the universe from the effects of sin so that a new heaven and a new earth will be established "in the dispensation of the fullness of times" (Eph. 1:10). He made possible his own reign and rule of authority at the right hand of the Father, and he will gather his redeemed people to his eternal kingdom to reign with him (2 Tim. 2:12). "He hath made us kings and priests and we shall reign on the earth" (Rev. 5:10). "If Christ is to be presented to men as a challenge to their thinking and living," Van Til observed, "he must be offered without compromise."[13] That uncompromising motif comes to prominence under the heading of Christ's cosmic significance, which can be considered in its several aspects.

Consider in the first place the salvation and eternal security of those whom Christ redeemed. In the wider terms now in view they were, by reason of the intratrinitarian communication and assignment, always entrusted to his care. That is so in the respect, first, that Christ was the agent of their creation. As the apostle Paul explained, it was by Christ, "the image of the invisible God ... [that] all things were created, that are in heaven, and that are in earth, visible and invisible ... all things were created by him, and for him" (Col. 1:15-16). But not only was Christ the agent of creation in accordance with the will of the Father. As Paul has there stated it, the entire

---

[12] See chap. 2 above.
[13] Van Til, *The Defense of the Faith*, 3.

creation was "for him" as well as "by him." That initial assignment of creation in time, or more precisely *into* time, points again to the end for which God created the world. Elevated there was the fact that in doing all that he has done, God the Father's objective was that the Son might be glorified. It was not only in his earthly assignment that the Father declared of the Son that "in him I am well pleased" (Matt. 3:17), or that he was referred to as "my beloved Son" (Luke 9:35). The intratrinitarian honor and mutual glorification existed eternally, before the beginning of time, and God's creation and redemptive designs proceeded in accordance with its terms and imperatives.

The biblical doctrine of the being of God requires us to say that the Persons of the Godhead are characterized by distinguishable properties. It is the distinguishable property of the Father that he generated the Son from all eternity. It is the distinguishable property of the Son that he was generated from the Father. The Son is the only begotten Son of the Father. That statement does not imply a lapse into a doctrine of divine subordinationism within the Godhead.[14] We hold firmly to the autotheotic nature of the Son and the Holy Spirit. They are fully God, as the Father is God. There is no subordination of Persons within the ontological Godhead, or the Godhead considered in its ontological aspect. It is proper and necessary to speak, of course, of an economic subordination of the Son to the Father, or a subordination in the discharge of the assigned and undertaken office of Messiah-redeemer. In that office and capacity Christ came, he said, to do the will of the Father. But he said with equal necessity and import that "I and my Father are one" (John 10:30). There is no subordina-

---

[14] The question of subordination within the Godhead has been variously treated in the theological literature. See Vickers, *The Fracture of Faith*, 67, and the reference there to the argument of Reymond regarding the supposed subordinationism of the Niceno-Constantinopolitan Creed and the discussion of Cunningham in his *Historical Theology*.

tion of, or between, the Father, the Son, and the Holy Spirit, regarded and worshipped as the ontological trinity.

In the mutual glorification of the Father and the Son, the work of creation was entrusted to the Son in order that he might have in his care, at all times and in all respects, those whom he had already agreed to bring to glory. But the process of redemption to which Christ had committed himself is understood more comprehensively when account is taken of the time dimension in which that process is being worked out. In that time process, the cosmic significance of Christ is expressed in the preservation of the world in order that those who were redeemed by Christ, including those still to be born, will come to him. That work of preservation in time is being effected by reason of God's sovereign providence and his eventuation of all of human history. And it is the Spirit of Christ, sent into the world from the Father, who is the agent of that preservation and operation. That immanent and providential working of God is subsumed, in terms of the biblical doctrine, under the rubric of God's common grace.

In that respect the second of the implications of the cosmic significance of Christ comes to prominence. That is that the doctrine of common grace is to be considered properly under the heading of the significance of the work of Christ. Common grace falls under the rubric of Christology. The work of Christ spreads its influence in preserving the world and human history until the full number of "Abraham's seed" have been brought to the realization of their redemption by Christ. Christ is the determiner and preserver of culture. It is by reason of Christ's redemptive assignment that the common grace of God is effective to the achievement of its divinely conceived objectives.

It follows that the cosmic significance of Christ extends not only to the preservation of the world in a bare or indifferent sense. At issue also is the fact that Christ's interest in the preservation and salvation of his people extends to his positive determination, by the operation of his common grace, of the entire history and development of human culture. What that involves is that God is at work eventuating the whole of human history in the interests of his church. That is the larger extent to which Christ, not only by his assumption of human nature but now by his immanent involvement in human history, has subjected himself to the context and passing of historical time.

We have spoken of Christ's involvement with his people, first in creation, and secondly in his administration of his grace in preserving them and bringing them to glory. He does that through the ministry of his Spirit, whom he had promised he would send and who, he said, would speak of him (John 15:26). The third respect in which the cosmic significance of Christ is to be observed has been clearly stated by the apostle Paul in his letter to the Ephesians. His statement bears directly and forcibly on the Christian's eschatological hope. There is, Paul said, a mystery in the will of God, aspects of which, however, have now been made clear (Eph. 1:9). God has established a purpose which he is bringing to full and final consummation in and by Christ. God has now "made known unto us the mystery of his will, according to his good pleasure which he hath purposed in himself ..."; and the description of that eschatological purpose follows: "That in the dispensation of the fullness of times he might gather together in one all things in Christ, both which are in heaven, and which are on earth, even in him" (Eph. 1:9-10).

The cosmic significance of Christ, Paul is saying, extends beyond the salvation of his people in any singular or isolated sense. Two more expansive realities are involved. First, the salvation of his people is now to be seen as a part of an extensive divine design whose objectives and implications extend to the re-creation and rehabilitation, the renewal and the eternal preservation, of all things. It is Christ who, by his work of redemption that has cleansed the universe of sin, makes possible God's ultimate establishment of the new heaven and the new earth. In and by him, as the Ephesian text has stated, all things will again be gathered together in one. In Ephesians 1:10 the Greek text uses one word which we have translated as "gather together in one." And that Greek word contains the prefix "ana" (ανα) which, in the compound word in which it appears, imports the sense of "again," or "by way of recapitulation." The statement being made is that in Christ all things will be gathered together "again." The implication is that all things were subject to disruption and decay by reason of Adam's fall. Not only was man himself subject to the disabilities, the deprivation and the depravation, that sin introduced. A generalized and universal disruption and decay occurred. "The creature [creation] was made subject to vanity ... [but] the creature [creation] itself also shall be delivered from the bondage of corruption [decay].... For we know that the whole creation groaneth and travaileth" (Rom. 8:20-22). Paul is saying that all things will again be restored to their primeval harmony, goodness, and beauty, and that by reason of the work of Christ that glorious eschatological terminus will be realized.

The more expansive implications of Christ's redemptive work have reference also to the fact that his redeemed people are now joined to him in a vital, organic, spiritual, and indissoluble union. They are thereby introduced to a union within a redeemed church that is Christ's property, in that it was given to him by the Father before the foundation of the world. It is in Christ that those who are redeemed by him are incorporated into the union of his church as indefectible members. He is the Head of the church he has redeemed. That establishes the organic dimension of our salvation. The Scriptures are replete with statements to that effect. "Christ loved the church," the same letter to the Ephesians states, "and gave himself for it" (Eph. 5:25). And it is the church which God in Christ has "purchased with his own blood" (Acts 20:28). Further, those realities establish the Christian's eschatological hope, in the respect that that hope is itself an organic expectation. The Christian has not only been redeemed as a personal and private entity, but he is being prepared for eternal participation in the prospective glorification of the church, into union with which he has been called.

A fourth aspect of the cosmic significance of Christ follows from his redemptive accomplishment. Christ came to be for the sinners he redeemed their substitute prophet, priest, and king. By reason of Adam's fall and his repudiation of his covenantal obligations we were constituted sinners (Rom. 5:12); and by virtue of the imputation to us of the guilt of his sin and the transmission to us of a fallen nature, we, like Adam, are disabled from fulfilling the demands of those initially mandated offices.[15] For that reason Christ, we have emphasized in an earlier chapter, came to do for us what we were unable to do for ourselves. But Christ now fulfills the office of king, as well as that of prophet and priest. That kingship is implicit in what has already been said regarding the reign and rule of Christ. He has been established by the Father in his position of authority in recognition of his faithful completion of his redemptive assignment. Christ rules as king, over the church that he has bought with his own blood (Acts 20:28), and over the entire reality external to the Godhead that God spoke into existence.[16]

A fifth aspect of the cosmic significance of Christ is significant for a Reformed theological apologetic. It rests in the fact that Christ has come into the world as the sinner's substitute prophet. That point of significance was addressed earlier when the meaning of the prophetic office was explored. It will be recalled that the essence of the prophetic office, as first mandated to Adam, was that of investigating, understanding, and explaining back to God the meaning of the

---

[15] The prophetic, priestly, and kingly offices to which Adam was at first mandated are discussed in Vickers, *Christian Confession*, chap. 5, and in chap. 2 above.

[16] An early discussion of the rule of Christ is contained in Geerhardus Vos, *The Teaching of Jesus Concerning The Kingdom and the Church* (Grand Rapids: Eerdmans, 1958).

reality-environment in which our first parents came to self-consciousness. God gave to Adam all necessary principles and categories of explanation. But those he lost in his false assertion of autonomy and his Fall. His false epistemological assertion was that he could find within himself, or within intramundane reality, or within a social context of opinion, all necessary principles of knowledge and criteria of truth and meaning. He did not need the principles of interpretation that God had at first communicated to him. But Christ has again disclosed to his people the true principles of understanding and the predication of meaning. Those know truly who know Christ truly. All things belong to Christ. All things and all that eventuates in human history are what they are, and they eventuate in the manner and in the structures they do, because Christ thought them before the foundation of the world. Christ established the laws of their being and function. All things are interpretable for the Christian only as they are interpreted Christologically. They have meaning only as they are interpreted as belonging to, and determined by, Christ.

The final aspect of cosmic significance returns us to the Colossian text we have cited. Christ is there said to have been the agent of the creation of all things. All things were created "*by* him" and "*for* him." It is in that way placed clearly before us that it was for the glory of Christ that all things have been brought to existence. All things exist and function now for his glory, and everything will minister to his glory in the ages to come. That, again, points to the reality that the end for which God has ordained all things is that his Son might be glorified. To him will be "glory for ever and ever" (Heb. 13:21).

All that exists is what it is because Christ thought it before the foundation of the world. All things belong to him. He is before all things, and in all things he has the preeminence. Because all of the facts of reality are his facts, and because they cohere and function by his created laws of being and operation, all things, and every aspect of reality, are to be interpreted by reference to him and his redeeming grace.

That, finally, is the extent of the cosmic significance of Christ and of what he has done in obedience to the Father's will. May God grant that we shall learn more perfectly to understand his grace to us, the laws of life that he has set before us, and the way of life that he calls us to live in obedience to him who has so graciously redeemed us from the entailment of our sin. For Christ is "Heir of all things." And he has called us to share that eternal inheritance with him.

Chapter 7

The Church:
Its Identity and Office

In the introduction to his important monograph, *The Imputation of Adam's Sin*, John Murray draws attention to the significant place in theological doctrine of the notion of solidarity. His immediate concern was with the fact of solidarity in sin and guilt in which the human race stands. That follows by reason of its solidarity with Adam, its federal head and representative, and from its implication in the guilt of Adam's first sin. Murray pointed out that the recognition of solidarity in the theological literature at the time he wrote did not accord, however, with the true realities of the human condition. "The recognition of and emphasis upon solidaric or corporate sin and guilt in our present-day theology are not to be interpreted as identical with the classic protestant doctrine of the imputation of Adam's sin."[1] Murray commented on the "mythical form in which the fact of solidaric unity in sin is expressed," and he dissented from the explanation in parts of the current literature of such critical texts as Romans 5:12-21.

---

[1] Murray, *The Imputation of Adam's Sin*, 6.

The reality of solidarity, however, remains. An appreciation of its relevance directs us to a biblically-consistent understanding of the human condition in two respects. First, it clarifies the bearing on that condition of our solidarity with Adam; and second, it elevates the contrary reality of the solidarity with Christ that those whom he redeemed enjoy. The latter brings to concrete expression a significant element of what we referred to in the preceding chapter as the cosmic significance of Christ. Our objective in this chapter is to investigate the relevance of that last-mentioned solidarity as it comes to expression in the doctrine of the church. Those whom Christ redeemed were once "in Adam" (1 Cor. 15:22), but now they have been moved by the grace of God from that Adamic state to a new solidarity in Christ.

That new solidarity comes to expression in individual life in a new existential status and relationship. The Holy Spirit's work of regeneration in the soul that turns the sinner to Christ involves and carries along with it the fact that he is now joined to Christ in a vital and indissoluble union. That union with Christ conveys to the individual the guarantee of all of the blessings and benefits that Christ purchased for him in his redemptive substitutionary life and death.

The reality that is involved has been put succinctly by the apostle Paul in his address to the elders of the Ephesian church. "Feed the church of God," he instructed them, "which he hath purchased with his own blood" (Acts 20:28). "Christ loved the church, and gave himself for it" (Eph. 5:25). The church that Christ gave himself to redeem is comprised of that countless number of people whom the Father had given to him for that redemptive purpose before the foundation of the world (John 17:6). Christ is now the Head of the church that he purchased, and it is in the church that the Christian believer's solidarity with Christ comes to expression. The organic nature of that union with Christ into which the Christian has been introduced points to his inclusion in the membership of the church. We referred to that in an earlier context when we contemplated the Christian's eschatological hope. That was seen to be an organic hope and expectation. That inheres in the fact that the Christian, who now participates in the organic entity of the church in this world in its visible aspect, will in that last great day share in the organic entity of the church redeemed. As members of Christ's redeemed church, true believers will reign with him. The believer's union with Christ is an organic union because he has been admitted to the organic entity of the church.

The church is to be considered in both its visible and its invisible aspects. In this chapter we shall consider principally, but not exclusively, the terms and status of the believer's membership of what may be referred to in short as the visible church. We are interested in the identity of the church in order to reflect on its office and function as God has appointed it in the world. The church in its visible aspect has been variously understood and described throughout the centuries. In some cultures it has been seen as a department of the state. A prominent example of that so-called Erastian form of church organization and government is found in Anglicanism in England. In some ecclesiastical cultures the opposite is held, and the state is understood to be a department of the church, as in Roman Catholicism. Within the wide limits of Protestantism different theories of church organization and government have existed. Some have emphasized a synodicalism, as in many Reformed and Presbyterian churches. Or one or the other of varying degrees of independency of church government has been prominent, as in English and American Congregationalism. But within the broad conspectus of Protestantism there has been a general uniformity of belief as to the meaning and responsibilities of church membership as we shall address it in what follows.

The visible church stands at this point in history in a unique position. It is unique in that the church has substantially surrendered the position of hegemony and cultural influence that it might once have enjoyed. The history of that devolution of influence need not detain us, and it is to be acknowledged that the church as the people of God has always had to stand against greater or lesser degrees of opposition, and even opprobrium in the eyes of the world, as it has pursued its mission of announcing the gospel of redemption. But now the church is substantially ignored for its irrelevance, if not despised for its meanness.

The indictment is to be laid against the church that it has to a large degree surrendered its own understanding of both its evangel and its mission in the world. A capitulation to the philosophic thought-forms of the age has diluted, if it has not destroyed completely, the doctrinal belief of the church, and a concession to the behavior norms of the world has blurred the distinctive culture of the church. What, it might be asked, is to be said of the church's kaleidoscope of rational theologies, its doctrineless ecumenicity, its turmoil in ecclesiastical form and worship, and its homiletical mediocrity?[2] One fears that the church has lost the battle, or is perilously in danger of doing so simply by falling prey to some of the shallowest fallacies of the age – the fallacies of imagining that it could hold an evangelism or an evangelicalism without the biblical evangel; that it could effectively preach the word of life and not be careful to hold the scriptural truths in scriptural proportion; that it could afford to bend to the behavior norms of the age and become careless in the handling of holy things; that it

---

[2] The indictment, that can be pursued at more length, has been addressed in several recent publications. I have discussed the contemporary stance of the church and have noted some recent evaluations from evangelical authors in *The Fracture of Faith*, chap. 1, where note is taken of the significant work of Mark A. Noll, *The Scandal of the Evangelical Mind* (Grand Rapids: Eerdmans, 1994), and the trilogy of David F. Wells, *No Place for Truth, or Whatever Happened to Evangelical Theology?; God in the Wasteland: The Reality of Truth in a World of Fading Dreams*; and *Losing Our Virtue: Why the Church Must Recover its Moral Vision* (Grand Rapids: Eerdmans, 1993, 1994, 1998).

could somehow accommodate the humanism of our time to the radicalism of scriptural diagnoses; or that doctrineless homilies could usefully replace honest exegesis and expository preaching in an age oppressed by uneven affluence and jealous of its comforts. We shall return to the relevant and important question of the extent to which a responsibility does or does not exist for the church to engage in contemporary social, cultural, and political affairs.

Our immediate concern is with the biblically-informed meaning and nature of the church and the benefits and obligations of membership within it. The subject raises some preliminary questions that deserve recognition.

Preliminary considerations

First, when we speak of church membership, it is the *church*, and not an autonomous social or cultural collectivity, of which we are speaking and of which we are members. It is the entity that God has established in this world as the institutional form in which he has chosen to administer his covenant of grace.

Second, we are seeking at this point a biblical-theological foundation of church organization and membership. What is required is not simply or only a "theological foundation," but, as has been said, a *biblical*-theological foundation. In this doctrineless age theology itself is at a discount. The church itself has to a large degree capitulated to a doctrineless ecumenicity. But theology, once the queen of the sciences, is still on churchmen's lips, though in its formation the imaginations of men have frequently replaced the thoughts of God. It is not true that any man's theology is as good as any other man's theology. In that direction lies the meaning, or rather the death of meaning, that characterizes the postmodernism that has been admitted to the church. To the contrary, the foundation for our subject must be clearly a *biblical-*theological foundation.

That statement stands on two basic premises. First, the church whose membership is being considered is the church of God. It is, in one expression, the church that God the Father gave to his Son to redeem in the divine articulation of the covenant of redemption. And in another expression it is the form of God's administration of that covenantal entity in the world and in history. Second, because our concern is addressed to the church of God, we are interested in what God has said about his church, and what, therefore, he has laid down in his Word regarding the scope, the purposes, the functions and responsibilities, and the prospects of it.

Third, we are concerned with the foundations of church membership as that applies to the church in both its invisible and its visible aspects. That, of course, introduces the important question of the relation that exists between those two aspects of the church. It will be necessary to reflect on the all-too-clear reality that not all regularly-admitted members of the church militant, or the visible church, are in fact true believers and thereby members of the church invisible. There have been in the past, as John recognized in his first epistle (1 John 2:19) and as the letter to the Hebrews acknowledged (Heb. 6:4-6), and there will undoubtedly be in the future, false professors among the true believers.

The church as the subject of the decree to redeem

The biblical doctrine of church membership traces back to a corresponding doctrine of God. It exists within the complex of doctrines that constitute a covenant theology. The divine covenantal purpose has been commented on in earlier contexts. At this time a single question is prominent: Who were the subjects of the eternal decrees that issued from God's predeterminate council? The answer bears vitally on two things directly relevant to our present discussion. First, it will clarify who it is that is legitimately a candidate for membership of the church; and second, it will throw its light on both the grounds on which such membership should be granted and the expectations which that carries with it.

For purposes of a minimal theological formulation, let us consider the threefold decrees of God: first, to elect a people, his church, to eternal salvation; second, to effect their redemption by the perfect obedience of his Son and his substitutionary atonement; and third, to call to himself in Christ those for whom Christ died. Before us are the decrees to elect (by God the Father), to redeem (by God the Son), and to call and sanctify (by God the Holy Spirit).

The subjects of each of those decrees were, in their individuality and particularity, the same in each case. The subjects of the decree to elect were those who were the subjects of the decree to redeem; and they were, again in their individuality and particularity, the subjects of the decree to call and sanctify. That statement needs to be made at the beginning of our doctrine of the church because it is denied by those who preach and teach a sub-biblical doctrine of the atonement. The evangelical church, to the extent that it is identified as Arminian or Amyraldian in its formulation of the gospel, differs from that designation of the subjects of the divine decrees. It has been seen that all such forms of sub-biblical theology point to a diminution of the doctrine of the unity and simplicity of God, by reason that they drive wedges between the works, the knowledge, and the being of the Father, the Son, and the Holy Spirit.[3]

God's covenantal administration

The subjects of the decrees to elect, to redeem, and to call which issued from the determinate council of the Godhead were by common designation a defined, numbered, particular, and unalterable set of people. That set of people were the common subjects of all of those salvific decrees. That, then,

---

[3] See chap. 6 above.

provides an initial response to the question of who are the members of the church. The church is made up of "the whole number of the elect." But our formulation has sharpened that doctrinal definition of the church. The church, focusing now on the membership of the church, is the set of people who were the common subjects of all of the divine salvific decrees.

But salvation, while it was designed and ordered outside of time by divine decree, was accomplished in actual historical time, and it is being applied and will be consummated in historical time. An adequate grasp of the meaning of the membership of the church requires, therefore, an understanding of God's administration in time of his covenant of grace.

We have adopted the terminology, God's "covenant of grace." That is done as a means of bringing into focus the necessary theological answer to the question of how the objectives of the eternal covenant of redemption were to be realized. To implement and consummate that covenantal design, God entered into a covenant with his people as they were represented by Christ, whereby he swore to effect their salvation and rescue them from the state to which Adam's fall had reduced them. How, then, does the progressive implementation of the covenant of grace throw its light on the meaning of the church and the membership of it?

That question addresses the successive forms of administration of God's covenant of grace. It takes up the administration of the church in its Old Testament form, or what is referred to in Acts 7:38 as "the church in the wilderness," and the church in its present form of administration in this age of grace. Running as a thread through our discussion from this point will be the relation between, and the distinction between, the church in its visible and its invisible aspects; or the visible and the invisible church respectively. The church invisible is made up of the elect true believers, those who are the subjects of the internal and effectual call of God by his Holy Spirit. The church visible is comprised of those who are externally called and who, professing faith in Christ, may or may not be true believers. Additionally, the church visible includes, along with all those who are thus externally called, their children who, therefore, are properly candidates for the reception of the initiatory rite of baptism into membership of the church. Those who are members of the visible church by external calling can be expected to include both true believers and the reprobate or false professors.[4]

The external and internal covenants

Reference has been made in the theological literature to God's *external covenant*, as that constitutes the administration of the church in its visible aspect, as distinct from his *internal covenant* with true believers.[5] The beneficiaries of the internal covenant are those who comprised that common set of fallen persons who were the subjects of the tripartite decree to elect, to redeem, and to call and sanctify.

Bannerman has established the relevant points as follows. "An outward Church, administered by human and fallible instruments, must necessarily share its benefits of a mere external kind with the feigned believer, as well as with the true.... It is for his sake [the true believer] that a visible Church, with its outward administration of word and ordinance, is established and kept up in the world. But side by side with the real Christian will be found the formal Christian also.... Such has been the condition of the Church in all ages, and such was it always intended to be."[6] Bannerman goes on to speak of the respect in which that relation between the subjects of the internal and the external covenants came to expression in earlier times. "Under a former economy there

---

[4] See Turretin, *Elenctic Theology*, 3:8-26.

[5] The concepts and terms of doctrine here under review are discussed in James Bannerman, *The Church of Christ*, (Edinburgh: Banner of Truth, 2 vols., 1960). See op. cit., 1:31.

[6] Ibid., 33.

were Church ordinances of an outward kind shared in by Israel after the flesh, no less than by Israel after the spirit – by the natural as well as the spiritual seed of Abraham. There was a church visible standing in an external relation to God, and embracing in it many who belonged to God only after the flesh; *and within the bosom of that external Church there was another, the invisible, standing in a spiritual relation to God, and embracing in it none but His spiritual people.* That former dispensation has passed away, and another has succeeded to it, of wider range and more elevated character. Yet *the principle of God's dealing with His people is still one and the same,* – God still provides for the benefit of His own believing people an outward framework, so to speak, of ordinances and external administration, *within which His invisible Church is hid.*"[7]

In that manner, Bannerman draws out at length the relations between, and the differences between, those members of the visible church who stand "in an inward and saving relationship to Christ" and those who stand "in an external relationship only."[8] Reference to God's *external* covenant envisages, first, the covenant that God made with the nation of Israel, whereby he separated them from all the other nations of the world to be his peculiar people. He did that, and he gave them his law, for a very special purpose. That is summed up by the apostle Paul in his letter to the Galatians, where he says that God gave his people his law as a "schoolmaster" to keep them separate from the other nations of the world who had fallen under the darkness of sin, and to preserve them in order that Christ should come from them (Gal. 3:24). That directs our thought to what is now referred to as the external covenant. It contained the promise of blessing for obedience as well as the promise of curse in the event of disobedience.

---

[7] Ibid., 33, italics added.
[8] Ibid., 34.

Within the scope and the structure of that external covenant there nestled what is referred to as the *internal* covenant. That refers to God's purpose of redemption in the sense that he preserved, within the larger confines of the nation with which he had covenanted, an inner core, or a special people, to whom, by the ministry of his Holy Spirit, he communicated a true faith and belief in the promise and the coming of Christ. But not all Israel were true to the obligations that God's covenant had placed upon them. Not all were true believers. Some were guilty of what are referred to in the Old Testament record as "presumptuous" sins, and they thereby forfeited the benefits of the promise of redemption (Num. 15:30-31; Deut. 17:2-7). Among the rest, not all were true or devout believers in the promise of redemption. Paul has put the same point clearly and beyond argument in his letter to the Romans, where he said that "they are not all Israel that are of Israel" (Rom. 9:6).

In the same way as there was an internal covenant that nestled within the broader external covenant that God had established with the nation of Israel, so now, as Bannerman has argued, a similar external-internal covenantal relation exists within the visible church in this time. As Peter has made clear, the church has replaced the nation in God's redemptive purpose (1 Peter 2:9). The church is now, Peter says, the "holy nation," repeating the very descriptive words that were previously applied to the nation of Israel (Ex. 19:6). In God's administration of his redemptive purpose in this in-between age, in the age of grace and of the church until Christ comes again, he has called into existence the church in its visible aspect or form. The church in its visible aspect is made up of all those who have made a credible or believable confession of faith in Christ, together with their children. The members of the church are professing believers. But it has been acknowledged that there are, and that there can be expected to be, false professors mixed among and within the body of true believers.

The point that has now to be made follows from what has just been said about the nation of Israel. In the same way as there existed an *external* covenant relation of God to the nation of Israel, so a corresponding *external* covenantal relation now exists between God and the church in its visible form. That is clear from a recognition of the benefits that follow from membership of the visible church, even to those who will in due course demonstrate themselves to have been false professors. Those benefits have to do with the privilege of hearing the gospel, of sharing in the external advantages of participating in the culture of the church, and of enjoying the aid and comfort of God's true people.

It follows also that within the broader limits and structure of the visible church God does have an inner core of true believers. That inner core of true believers are the called people of God with whom he has entered into what is referred to as the *internal* covenant. They are numbered among his elect. That internal covenant comes to expression in the lives and histories of its true beneficiaries, in the same way as there was, in Israel of old, a corresponding *internal* covenantal people existing within the wider confines of the nation that enjoyed the benefits of the external covenant.

The writer to the Hebrews has said (Heb. 10:29) that it is "the blood of the covenant," which the false professors and apostates treat as a "common" or "unholy" thing, that has made possible the entire form and history of the church. It is the blood of Christ that has made it possible for both the *external* (the visible church in its general aspect) and the *internal* (the body of true believers within the visible church) to come to visible and historical expression.

The conditions of entry to church membership

Two questions follow from all that has been said. First, what is it that establishes one a member of the true church of Christ, or of the church considered in its invisible aspect? As that question is not our primary concern at this point, we can put the answer briefly. It follows from our discussion of the eternal divine decrees that the membership of the church in its invisible aspect was established, definitively and unalterably, when, in giving expression to the decree of redemption, their names were written in the book of life before the foundation of the world (Rev. 13:8; 17:8). The membership of the church invisible includes "the whole number of the elect that have been, are, or shall be gathered into one, under Christ the head thereof; and is the spouse, the body, the fulness of him that filleth all in all."[9] Now, in time, those elect for whom Christ died are brought to the state of repentance and saving faith by the renewing, regenerating work of the Holy Spirit, who has committed himself to apply to them all of the benefits of the redemption that Christ accomplished, to sanctify them wholly, and to conduct them to glory.

The second question concerns the condition of entry to membership of the church in its visible aspect. The single necessary qualification for membership is a visible, credible, or believable, profession of belief of the gospel and of repentance from sin and faith in Christ. If such a profession is made, then the church, in the persons of its elders and with the concurrence of the members, is permitted and required to admit to membership the person making such a profession. But in connection with that, two things are to be said.

First, the profession of faith must be understood to be credible, or believable, only if there are no demonstrable reasons to conclude that the life of the applicant for membership is inconsistent with his or her profession. What is professed in words cannot be contradicted in fact. That, admittedly, calls for careful discrimination on the part of the examining elders of the church. Secondly, admission to membership of the church is to be understood in the light of what has been said regarding God's administration of an

---

[9] Westminster Confession of Faith, XXV, I.

external, as distinct from an internal, covenant with the church. It follows, as has been said, that as the New Testament Scriptures have made abundantly clear, there will be false professors among the membership of the church.

That, however, has been denied at some points in the history of the theology of the church. It is not necessary to discuss more fully at this point the respects in which Roman Catholic theology has denied the distinctions we have drawn between the church in its visible and its invisible aspects. But it is probably of more interest to observe that in some expressions of what might loosely be called "Independency," as that connotes a form of church polity, the view has been held that the local church is made up of truly called and regenerate believers. Quite apart from some modern-day instances, the movement of English independency in the nineteenth century frequently took such a position. The work of Ralph Wardlaw on Congregational Independency, for example, argued that a true saving work of grace in the soul was the only ground or condition of church membership.[10] But that denies the distinctions between God's *external* and *internal* covenants in his administration of the church in this time. Moreover, the suggestion contained in it, that the local church is to be regarded as a called company of true believers, in effect arrogates to the examining eldership a prerogative which, under the Scriptures, they do not possess. For they would be required, under the conditions envisaged, to judge regarding the definitive state of soul of the candidate for membership. Such a position, further, effectively denies the difference between the visible and the invisible church. That alone destroys its scripturicity, having regard to what has been revealed regarding God's administration in history of his covenant of grace and the formal structure of the church in the light of it.

---

[10] See the extensive historical review in Bannerman, *The Church of Christ*, 1: 73ff.

The preparatory work of the Holy Spirit

So far as the theological foundations of our subject are concerned, two remaining questions bear with some immediacy on the question of church membership. If the church in its visible expression has historically included, and if it can be expected in this time to include, false professors as well as true believers, it is of some interest to ask why that should be so. The answer to that question requires us to consider what is to be referred to as "the preparatory work of the Holy Spirit."

A survey of the Scriptural data makes it clear that there can and does take place in the soul of an individual a work of the Holy Spirit that may proceed to a very remarkable extent, and yet leave that individual in an unregenerate state (Heb. 6:4-6). The primary appeal of the gospel, or the real point of contact that the gospel makes with the unbeliever, rests in the fact that every person has, within the recesses of his soul, an ineradicable conviction that God exists and has a claim on his obedience. The *sensus deitatis* (sense of Deity) is embedded in the soul by virtue of the fact that man is, and that he remains in spite of his sin, the image of God. God has kept open the channels of communication to him (Rom. 1:18ff). The mysterious dealing of the Holy Spirit, beyond the awakening of the *sensus deitatis*, remains subject to the sovereign dispensation of God in the light of his eternal covenant of redemption, and no person has, or could ever have had, any claim on God's mercy and grace. The extent of God's awakening conviction of sin in the soul of an individual, the extent to which the person's attention and interest might or might not be turned to recognize the claims of God, remain subject to divine providence, not to external human inspection.

The fact that individual persons may be brought to a profession of faith in Christ which nevertheless is subsequently demonstrated to have been a false profession is the argument in the sixth chapter of the letter to the Hebrews. The apostle John, in his first epistle, was acutely conscious of the same reality and problem. In his reference to false professors, who had actually enjoyed the communion and hospitality of the true church, he states that "they went out from us, but they were not of us; for if they had been of us, they would no doubt have continued with us; but they went out, that they might be made manifest that they were not all of us" (1 John 2:19). And of course, the case of Judas again instances the point. In his High Priestly prayer our Lord stated that "those that thou gavest me I have kept, and none of them is lost, but the son of perdition" (John 17:12). Judas was lost. But he was the son of perdition. He was always the son of perdition. He was never anything other than the son of perdition, though he had enjoyed the company and shared in the spiritual gifts of the true believers.

In the letter to the Hebrews remarkable statements are made regarding those who recanted from their profession of faith and, having apostatized, demonstrated that their earlier profession had been false. They were those, it is said, "who were once enlightened, and have tasted of the heavenly gift, and were made partakers of the Holy Ghost, and have tasted the good things of the word of God, and the powers of the world to come" (Heb. 6:4-5). It is further said of such apostates in the tenth chapter of the same letter that they "have received the knowledge of the truth," but that then they have "trodden under foot the Son of God, and have counted the blood of the covenant wherewith [they were] sanctified an unholy thing, and have done despite unto the Spirit of God" (Heb. 10:26-29).

The point at issue is that the people referred to have had the benefit of a work of the Spirit of God in their lives, they have made a statement of repentance, which, however, has subsequently proved to have been a false repentance, and yet, at the end of the Spirit's work they have remained unregenerate. The relevant point of doctrine is, accordingly, twofold.

First, the Holy Spirit of God is sovereign in his work and ministry in the souls of individuals. His work may proceed to a very considerable and remarkable extent, and yet, at the end, he may not consummate his work by conveying the grace of regeneration. The individual may remain still in the realm of darkness and the kingdom of Satan. But it may well be the case, and in the mercy of God it is frequently the case, that at the end of that preparatory work of the Spirit the individual is blessed with the sovereign grace and gift of regeneration. The gift of faith is bestowed. Those who have been made regenerate come to Christ. There are no regenerate unbelievers; the regenerate believe; and there are no unregenerate believers.

Second, we come, finally, to the significance of all this for the decision that must be made by the church, operating through its ruling and teaching elders, in the matter of admission to membership. After having observed what there is every reason to believe is a true work of the Spirit of God, and having received an applicant's testimony of faith that there is no reason to judge is contradicted by any inconsistency of life, such an applicant should be admitted to membership. If, in due course, the profession should prove to have been false and the credibly-admitted member apostatizes, the church will nevertheless have acted properly in its previous decision.

What has been said by way of explanation of the Spirit's work given in the letter to the Hebrews does not, however, have the agreement of all Reformed scholars. R. C. Sproul has argued that the individuals contemplated in the sixth chapter of that letter are to be understood as regenerate people. His argument, which runs counter to a long line of Reformed opinion, can be inspected in his *Grace Unknown: The Heart of Reformed Theology*.[11] Sproul is influenced by the statement in the text that the individuals referred to had come to "repentance." He has failed to see that the statement that it is "impossible ... to renew them again to repentance" refers to the fact that no amount of reasoned argument is able to renew

---

[11] R. C. Sproul, *Grace Unknown: The Heart of Reformed Theology* (Grand Rapids: Baker, 1997), 213ff.

them even to the position of the false repentance they had previously made. For that reason, the writer of the letter turns away from such people and their condition in order to proceed with his exposition of positive doctrine, in particular that of the high priesthood of Christ, to those who he has reason to believe on the grounds of charity are true believers.

The obligations of church membership

What, finally, are the obligations that membership of the church places upon the individual? The answer follows from what has been said regarding membership of the true church, considered in its invisible aspect. Peter, in the context of his explanation that the church is now the "holy nation," goes on to state that the objective of it all is that those who are professing members of the church, "should show forth the praises of him who has called [them] out of darkness into his marvellous light" (1 Peter 2:9). And Paul has made the point repeatedly. God has chosen us "in Christ," he explained to the Ephesians, "that we should be holy and without blame before him ... to the praise of the glory of his grace" (Eph. 1:4,6).

"Be ye holy," Peter says, repeating the injunction of Leviticus 11:44, and "as he which hath called you is holy, so be ye holy in all manner of conversation" (1 Peter 1:15-16). At the end of his second epistle Peter counsels the true believing members of the church that Christ redeemed, "Grow in grace and in the knowledge of our Lord and Savior Jesus Christ" (2 Peter 3:18). The exhortations could be multiplied.

The members of God's true church have been called to a new solidarity, a union with one another, that derives from our union with Christ. We are individuals, but we do not live and behave in the church individualistically. We have the high privilege of suffering together when one suffers and rejoicing together when one rejoices. "We, being many, are one body in Christ, and every one members one of another" (Rom. 12:5; see also 1 Cor. 12:25-27).

The office of the church

The church is the custodian of God's revelation. Its office and function in its visible manifestation are determined by that basic awareness. To the church God has entrusted the Word of life. To it have been given the keys of the kingdom. To his disciples Christ said, "I will give unto thee the keys of the kingdom of heaven; and whatsoever thou shalt bind on earth shall be bound in heaven; and whatsoever thou shalt loose on earth shall be loosed in heaven" (Matt. 16:19). The church, by reason of its possession of the Word of God, is charged to make clear to all men everywhere the conditions on which rescue and relief from the entailment of sin is possible. The call to repentance and the announcement of the forgiveness of sin goes out from the church and declares that salvation is freely available to all who turn to Christ in repentance and faith.[12] In his comment on the text Calvin observes that "there is no other way in which the gate of life is opened to us than by the word of God." The church is to state the criteria for entrance to life eternal that the Word of God has declared.

It is not being said at this point that the church as an institution in the world has authority to dispense forgiveness of sin apart from its announcement of the invitation to Christ that is replete in the gospel. The underlying Greek text at the words translated as "bound" and "loosed" in Matthew 16:19 contains the verbs in the perfect tense. That indicates that what is "bound on earth" on earth "will have been bound in heaven," and what is "loosed on earth," by reason of repentance as that is called for in the gospel, "will have been loosed in heaven." The dispensation of salvation, as that follows upon the faithful preaching of the church, will be to those true believers who are brought to their confession by the work of the Holy Spirit within the soul. In that work, the Spirit is applying to those

---

[12] See John Murray, "The Free Offer of the Gospel," *Collected Writings*, 4:113-132.

individuals the gifts and benefits that Christ purchased for them in his atoning death. They are the ones whom the Father chose to redeem before the foundation of the world. Coming to confluence, then, is the work of the Father, the Son, and the Holy Spirit in the accomplishment and application of salvation for God's people. The church, when it is true to its calling and faithful in its testimony, will be the instrument in God's grace and purpose in bringing to consummation his redemptive objectives. Paul reminded Timothy of the same privilege, and the responsibility and obligation it carries with it, when he wrote, "preach the word" (2 Tim. 4:2).

It is correct to say that there is no salvation outside of the church. But such a statement simply brings to expression the implication of what was said in the preceding discussion; namely, that the church is the church of the redeemed saints of God, and it is accordingly within the church that those who are effectually called to salvation in this life reside. Those who come to Christ do so because they have been ordained as members of the church in its invisible aspect. They are therefore to be welcomed within, and they are obligated to seek admission to, the church in its visible aspect. It is within the church that the community of God's people are to be found, sharing the unique culture of the church as distinct from the culture of the world, and sharing the same hope and eschatological expectation.

Beyond the office of the church in preserving the deposit of truth that God has given in his Word and announcing the invitation of the gospel to all men everywhere, two further obligations are placed upon it. The first has to do with the nurture of the saints that have been admitted to the church. The second has to do with the relation of the church to the wider culture outside the church. The latter concerns the extent to which the church may properly pronounce upon, or attempt to contribute to the resolution of, external social and cultural issues.

The first of these matters directs us to the proper understanding of what God has declared in his Word regarding the administration of the church. At this point only a minimal observation need be made. The form of organization and administration of the visible church may be observed by a careful review of the New Testament record. Instruction to that end is found, first, in the explicit teaching contained in the apostolic literature; second, in the apostolic examples as to the procedures they adopted and the arrangements for the government of the church they implemented; and third, from what, as the Westminster Confession judiciously states, "by good and necessary consequence may be deduced from scripture."[13] Suffice it to say that the apostles "ordained elders in every church" (Acts 14:23), and the comparable instruction was conveyed to Titus, "For this cause left I thee in Crete, that thou shouldest ... ordain elders in every city, as I had appointed thee" (Titus 1:5). The church is to be governed by duly ordained officers who are called by Christ and appointed for that purpose. The elders of the church are not the servants of, or the messengers for, what might be interpreted as the democracy of the church membership. The church is not a democracy. It is a constitutional monarchy over which Christ rules as Head, and over which he has appointed elders as governors to rule as his regents.

When Paul was returning from his missionary journey and called the elders of the Ephesian church to meet with him he gave them the instruction, "Take heed therefore unto yourselves, and to all the flock, over which the Holy Ghost hath made you overseers, to feed the church of God, which he hath purchased with his own blood" (Acts 20:28). The primary duty and function of the elders whom Christ has called and appointed to rule his church are observable in that statement. The elders are primarily responsible for the nurture of the saints. That nurture involves the careful watch over the saints' progress in sanctification and their cultivation of

---

[13] Westminster Confession of Faith, I, VI.

the means of grace to that end. It involves also the protection of the church from the heresies and arguments against the truth of God that attack the Christian confession. Of urgent concern at the present time is the need for the ordained leaders of the church to counter the false teaching that has been referred to as the "openness of God," or the claims of "open theism" that have invaded and misdirected contemporary evangelicalism.[14] The qualifications for the office of elder that Paul subsequently laid down clearly point to the effective discharge of that responsibility and obligation (1 Tim. 3:1f.; Titus 1:6f.).

The extent of the church's prerogative in its relation with the world outside the church has been variously understood. When Paul said to Timothy, "Preach the word" (2 Tim. 4:2), he was defining the principal and the only duty and responsibility of the church. By that it is meant that the duty of the church is to preserve and declare the gospel, to announce that "Christ Jesus came into the world to save sinners" (1 Tim. 3:15). Whatever else the church does or may properly do is to be done in the context of its preaching the Word and is to be consistent with it. That essential focus of the church's mandate and responsibility precludes it from participating directly in matters of governmental, industrial, or social policy in relation to which there is no reason to believe the church has any competence. In that respect a distinction is to be drawn between the prerogatives and responsibilities of the church as the church, and those of Christian men as Christian men. It is the privilege and responsibility of the latter to bring to bear on their spheres of influence the imperatives of the Christian faith as they are relevant to questions of social and political interest. But specific policy issues and questions are beyond the mandate of the church as the church.

That does not mean that the church has nothing to say

---

[14] See the discussion of open theism and its doctrinal misconceptions in chap. 4 above.

about matters of important social concerns. It would be improper, for example, for the church to state and advise that the minimum wage in the United States should be raised to a certain specified level. But it is entirely proper for the church to make clear the biblical teaching regarding the obligations of employers to deal equitably with employees, and for the latter to be diligent in discharging their contractual obligations. The church is obligated to bring to bear on social discourse the biblical principles that govern human relations, principles of equity, fairness, and honesty in dealing. That is saying in other words that the church should state in clear terms the biblical mandates that are relevant to social, cultural, and political issues, without trespassing on grounds that clearly require technical competence that the church or the ministers of the church do not possess.

To take a case or two in point: the church may properly make clear the biblical principles that deny the right of abortion on demand, without engaging in or sponsoring civil disturbance in that cause. It may articulate biblical principles that contradict inequities and corruption in corporate management, without specifying what actual levels of remuneration should apply in particular situations. On the grounds of human solidarity and equity the church may declare opposition to all forms of social, industrial, and political discrimination. In the interest of biblical principles of equity it may take note of the extremes of income and wealth distribution that exist in some industrial and market economies, and on the fact that governmental taxation policies may contribute to those distributions, without specifying what precise levels of either distributions or taxation policies should exist.

The church may announce the principles of equity that God so clearly enunciated through the Old Testament prophets when he spoke vehemently against the maltreatment and exploitation of the poor and the economically disadvantaged. "The earth is the Lord's" (Ps. 24:1), "The silver is mine, and the gold is mine, saith the Lord of hosts" (Hag. 2:8), "For every beast of the forest is mine, and the cattle upon a thousand hills" (Ps. 50:10), and it is for those reasons that God has given us guidance in his Word regarding the preservation and administration of what belongs to him. The Lord has regard to the poor, "The rich and the poor meet together; the Lord is maker of them all" (Prov. 22:2); and the charge of exploitation of the poor is explicitly brought by the prophet Amos, "Hear this, O ye that swallow up the needy, even to make the poor of the land to fail, saying, When will the new moon be gone, that we may sell corn ... making the ephah small and the shekel great, and falsifying the balances by deceit? That we may buy the poor for silver, and the needy for a pair of shoes" (Amos 8:4-6). Excessive concentrations of economic power and the exploitation of those concentrations to the disadvantage of other members of society are forthrightly condemned. "Woe unto them that join house to house, that lay field to field, till there be no place, that they may be placed alone in the midst of the earth" (Is. 5:8). A fuller discussion would disclose the extensive guidance, as to the relevant principles involved, that are available to us in the Word of God for social and economic administration.[15]

In short, it is the privilege and prerogative of the church as the church to declare that Christ is king over all, and that the principles of order and human relations that his Word conveys should govern in all areas of social conduct. As to the points at which the voice of the church may intervene in the public square, attention should be paid to the mandate of the moral law as "summarily comprehended in the Ten Commandments,"[16] and the imperatives that those commandments project should be claimed to be operative. Because, for

---

[15] A copious literature exists on these and related questions. See my *A Christian Approach to Economics and the Cultural Condition* (Smithtown, N.Y.: Exposition Press, 1982). Insightful discussions are contained in John Murray, *Principles of Conduct* (Grand Rapids: Eerdmans, 1957).

[16] Westminster Shorter Catechism, Question 41.

example, the sixth commandment says, "Thou shalt not kill," the church is required and obligated to state that abortion as generally understood in modern cultures is murder. Because the eighth commandment says, "Thou shalt not steal," and because the tenth commandment says, "Thou shalt not covet," the church may state that obscene inequities in income and wealth distribution are not consistent with the biblical desiderata. Because the fourth commandment says, "Remember the Sabbath day, to keep it holy," the church may state its objection to the widespread desecration of that day in industrial, governmental, and social functioning.

It may be rejoined in those connections that whereas the moral law is the province of the church, for the ordering and governing of personal lives, it is beyond the prerogative of the church to project its mandates in the manner proposed to the wider social sphere. But such a rejoinder is clearly without merit. For the moral law, as it was written and codified in the Decalogue, is to be understood as a republication and rearticulation of the law of life that God gave to our first parents at the creation. The moral law is to be seen as a reflection of God's own holiness and perfections. It is for that reason that it is the rule of life for all men everywhere at all times.

The Christian church is set to be the salt of the earth and light in the darkness in which the world is enshrouded in sin. Its impact on the culture of the times is in an important respect to be an indirect impact and influence. The church discharges its mission and fulfills its mandated office when its clear and truthful announcement of the gospel is allowed to work its uncluttered effects in the souls of all those who will hear. The church is not expected to surrender its own unique culture for the culture of the world. It is not to give hospitality to the thought-forms of the world, the idioms in speech or music of the world, or the wider behavior norms and lifestyles of the world, in the mistaken hope that it will thereby be more attractive to the man of the world. In this day of cultural decay, when the church is largely ignored for its seeming irrelevance, it is to be hoped that more hearers will be attracted to the church to hear the Word of life. But it should be borne in mind that the man of the world will never be attracted to the church because the church is made more like the world. He will be attracted to the church only when, and because, he is able to see that the life and culture of the people in the church are different from that of the world.

The directives of Paul to the Colossians, "Walk in wisdom toward them that are without," that are outside the church (Col. 4:5), and to the Thessalonians, "Walk honestly toward them that are without" (1 Thess. 4:12), and the directive of Peter, "Sanctify the Lord God in your hearts; and be ready always to give an answer to every man that asketh you a reason of the hope that is in you with meekness and fear" (1 Peter 3:15), provide guidance to what should be the character of the Christian life before the world. May God grant that we his people shall learn more perfectly to understand and follow the guidance for life that he has graciously given us in his Word. Then we shall learn to "do all to the glory of God" (1 Cor. 10:31).

Chapter 8

The Issues Revisited

The critical and evaluative literature has made it a commonplace to observe that not all is well with the church. The uncertainty of its testimony within, and the cultural confusions of the age without, have coalesced to diminish the ability of the church to serve any longer as a cementing element in social cohesion. The time when even a soulless nod of respectability was accorded to church-going is past. Culture is blatantly, if not proudly, godless now. Old landmarks no longer rein personal consciences. Human life is cheapened, by abortion at its source, by its ill-thought clamor for scientific structuring of its form, and by its willingness to submit to euthanasia in its termination. The vicissitudes of war and the pressures of economic deprivations have sapped social confidences. But the church rings out only an uncertain sound. Its testimony is muted. It is intimidated by changing fashions of philosophic opinion, and its erstwhile evangel has been compromised to irrelevance and ineffectiveness. The churches are either empty, or in their mega-form have frequently only a pseudo-gospel to declare. David Wells has pointedly asked why there is now "No place for truth," and his question, "Whatever happened to evangelical theology?" strikes to the heart of both the present discontent and the identification of its cause.[1]

The questions with which we began persist. Why is the contemporary condition what it is? Why does the church speak with only an uncertain voice, seemingly unsure of its sounder heritage, in veiled betrayal of the deposit of truth entrusted to it? Why has it all too often nothing to say by way of diagnosis of the human condition? Have we forgotten beyond recall the truth for which the fathers of the church lived and died? Has the church sold its birthright for an evanescent mess of cultural pottage? What, in the end, has been accomplished by the church's cultural accommodations in its behavior norms and its philosophic accommodations in its pseudo-evangel? Is theology cheapened at a discount that points to final abandonment, beyond the possibility of sensible recovery? We have endeavored to trace in the preceding chapters the essence, some aspects of its content, and the relevance of that "faith once delivered to the saints" (Jude 3) that bears on the answers.

The contemporary condition is in vital respects no different from what it has been since the beginning. Human nature remains shackled by the realities of the sinful condition inherited from Adam's fall. A widening of existential possibilities has come from scientific, technological, literary, and all forms of artistic cultural advance. But that very expansion has bred a barrenness of soul. Science and morality are in conflict. Art too often mocks the ordinary living of life. The cisterns from which we have been asked to drink have proved to be broken. Their waters fail. The thirst of soul is not slaked. And in its demeaned condition the church is seemingly bereft of an understanding of the true state of affairs.

But two realities still lie in juxtaposition. The first we

---

[1] Wells, *No Place for Truth Or Whatever Happened to Evangelical Theology?*

have just adumbrated as the contemporary condition. The second is that the gospel of the grace of God remains true and relevant if only we strain to recapture it. The God of heaven who sent his Son to be the Savior of sinners continues to work out his eternal designs. Our redeemer-king, the Lord Jesus Christ, continues to fulfill his promise that he will build his church and the gates of hell shall not prevail against it (Matt. 16:18). Certain it is that God moves in a mysterious way, and that the clouds we so easily dread are big with blessing.[2] Certain it is that Christ will preserve his church. The eternal covenant by which God has sworn to bring his saints to the inheritance reserved for them has not been annulled. The saints of God have reason to believe that in the longer horizon the future of their status is secure. The Word of God remains, not only as the true diagnosis of every aspect of the human condition, but as the way of life for all times and all people everywhere, and as the assurance that the purpose and promises of God will be fulfilled.

It is not necessary to retrace the argument of the preceding chapters in detail to bring to sober judgment the questions they have raised. The questions themselves return us to the theological doctrines with which we began. First, the question that engaged Athanasius persists. The rolling ages since and their advancing sophistication have dulled neither the insistence nor the urgency of the question, "Who is Jesus Christ?"

Our Lord on one occasion tested public opinion and his disciples' awareness of it by asking, "Whom do men say that I the Son of man am?" (Matt. 16:13). The answers were various. Some said he was John the Baptist, or Elijah, or some other prophet. And when the question was pressed as to who the disciples themselves understood their master to be, Peter responded with the inspired declaration that here in their

---

[2] See William Cowper, *Light Shining out of Darkness*, in Donald Davie, ed., *The New Oxford Book of Christian Verse* (Oxford: Oxford University Press, 1981), 198-99.

midst was "the Christ, the Son of the living God" (Matt. 16:16). Again, after Christ had fed the five thousand by his miracle of expanding the five loaves and two fishes, he had cause to ask his disciples whether they too, as did many at that time, would leave him because of the directness and penetration of his teaching. Peter again voiced the response of the inner circle of followers. "Lord, to whom else shall we go? Thou hast the words of eternal life. And we believe and are sure that thou art that Christ, the Son of the living God" (John 6:67-69). But such a clarity of conviction no longer exists. The world is still divided as to what the answer to that question of all the ages is, or should be. And the church holds only uncertainly to the apostles' early testimony.

The question remains: Who is Jesus Christ? Let us retrace the argument briefly. Are we to say that, after all, some truth may lie in the claim of Arius? Was the man Jesus Christ who suffered and hungered in this world, who thirsted for a drink of water from the woman at the well of Samaria, who ate with sinners and healed their diseases, merely a human person? The Christian confession has claimed that a human body and a human nature were created for our Lord's assumption of them into union with his divine nature. But it has claimed also that here we confront a mystery. In this man Jesus Christ two natures are joined in union in one person, two natures between which there is no communication of properties. Peter's confession was the early Christian claim. Jesus Christ was not a human person. He was not a "human being," as some theologians have begun to say in apparent accommodation to the unisex demand of the age.[3] Jesus Christ was not a "human person" or a "human being." Nor was he a divine-human person, partly divine and partly human in his personhood in a sense that it would be necessary then to unravel. Jesus Christ was a divine being, a divine Person.

---

[3] See Robert A. Peterson, Sr., *Calvin and the Atonement* (Fearn, Scotland: Christian Focus Publications, Mentor imprint, 1999), 25, 32.

Are we to say that the claim of Arius was correct in its essence? How could there ever have been any entry into time of a divine Person? If time was itself a creation of God it must forever remain outside of God, impenetrable by God. If that was not so, God's eternal separateness would be destroyed and his transcendence negated. If time was itself eternal, then it must be forever in correlation with God, separable and distinct from him. Is there not cogency in the Gnostic claim that matter and spirit, evil and good, cannot possibly come into existent union? Perhaps Arius was on good grounds in saying that Jesus Christ was a creature of a superior God. Perhaps Sabellius is to be credited with unusual insight in saying that what trinitarian Christianity saw as three Persons in the Godhead was to be understood as simply three different manifestations or emanations of the one God. Perhaps docetic Gnosticism was correct to discern that the man Jesus Christ possessed only a phantom body, that he was a person on whom the Spirit of God came but departed from at the time of his death.

The rejection of all such heresies in the years preceding the Council of Chalcedon in 451 and the consolidation at that time of the church's Christological confession have informed subsequent theological and doctrinal orthodoxy. The achievement of the protestant Reformation in the sixteenth century speaks eloquently to that effect. But doctrinal deterioration in later times has tarnished the church's professed belief. Jesus Christ, it is now being asserted, was less than the eternal Son of God. His incarnation is called in question. His resurrection is thought to be unbelievable. The ethical imperatives of Christianity, it is now being said, are supportable without insistence on the minutiae of Christian dogma. The homilies of the church too often mount a direct address to what is perceived as the psychological needs of its congregation, to the dismissal of radical diagnoses that the Scriptures provide. Sin has lost its terror, because the holiness of God has been discounted. Redemption is in the last analysis imagined to be dependent on one's own sovereignty and competence. Assumptions of human autonomy are now in fashion.

Consider, secondly, Augustine's question. Against the preceding question, "Who is Jesus Christ?" it is now to be asked, "What is man?" If, as the Scriptures have declared, man is the image of God, is he in any sense liable for the curse that Adam sustained as his federal head and representative? Does he bear any liability in relation to the guilt of unfulfilled covenantal obligations that fell heavily on his first parents? Does he continue to be the image of God (Gen. 9:6; James 3:9) and to sustain the responsibilities and obligations which that identity implies? Does liability for sin and the disabilities that sin connotes devolve on him now that he is so far removed in time from Adam's dereliction? If that should in any respect be so, is it true to say that not only is his mind now darkened by the god of this world, but that his will is weakened beyond the capacity to perform any action to eternal good and spiritual worth?

It is not necessary to recall in detail what has been said regarding the status of the will as a result of Adam's fall. The reduction of Christianity to the pale form that it occupies in its semi-Pelagian dimensions is clear in the neo-Arminianism of the evangelical church. What we have inspected as the biblical doctrine of reciprocal imputation, the imputation of the sinner's guilt to Christ and that of the righteousness of Christ to the repentant sinner, has fallen from consistent recognition. The present condition of belief in that connection accords with John Murray's comment on the influential claim of Dodd half a century ago. Dodd concludes that "Paul's doctrine of Christ as the 'second Adam' is not so bound up with the story of the Fall as a literal happening that it ceases to have meaning when we no longer accept the story as such. Indeed, we should not too readily assume that Paul did so accept it."[4] Modern theology drastically rewrites the apostolic

---

[4] Murray, *The Imputation of Adam's Sin*, 5.

attestation of the truth as it has been revealed in and by Christ and as it is enshrined in his Word.

Perhaps the Synod of Dordt erred to an excess in its rejection of the Pelagianism that attacked the Reformation soteriological statement. Perhaps the counter-Reformation and the deliverances of the Roman Catholic Council of Trent rehabilitated the pristine Christian truth. Perhaps the mediating theology of Amyraldianism should be accorded a higher place in the reconciliation of post-Reformation divergent trends of belief. Perhaps Pelagius saw things more clearly when he said that man is responsible for his own sin, not in any sense the guilt of Adam's first sin, because the reality is that he simply sins in the same sense as Adam did and after his example. The situation may be as Brunner saw it when he stated in his exegesis of Romans 5:12, "It does not refer to the transgression of Adam in which all his descendants share; but it states the fact that 'Adam's' descendants are involved in death, because they themselves commit sin."[5]

The testimony of the Word of God, however, "the faith which was once delivered unto the saints" (Jude 3), stands against all such accommodating imaginations and suggestions. But again the contemporary church is called to respond to a damaging indictment. As it has, in the preceding regard, frequently held a view of Christ that is too low when measured against the biblical revelation, now its view of man is higher than what that Scriptural disclosure warrants. Again the realities are that because the church has lost the biblical doctrine of sin it has pointed men to the mistaken conception that they possess all abilities of will, if only they will realize it and act accordingly, to save themselves.

The third of the questions that compel an answer is that of Anselm. Is it true to say that the only sustainable meaning projected by the death of Jesus Christ is that in his dying he provided the sufficient and acceptable satisfaction for the sins

---

[5] Quoted in Murray, ibid., 5.

of his people? Perhaps the claims of accommodating theology as to the meaning of Christ's atonement are worthy of higher merit than doctrinal orthodoxy has accorded them. Perhaps the essential significance of Christ's death rests simply in its demonstration that punishment of sin is inherent in God's government of the universe. Perhaps Anselm's "satisfaction theory" of the atonement should be replaced by a "governmental theory." Or perhaps a so-called "moral theory," of the kind held by the seventeenth-century Socinians, should take the place of both. The sole objective of the death of Christ, on that latter view of things, is to exert a moral effect upon the sinner.[6] Perhaps the doctrine that in his death Christ provided "a ransom for many" (Mark 10:45; Matt. 20:28) misconstrues his own conception of the demands of his messianic assignment. Perhaps what has been claimed as orthodox doctrine has erred in its claim that the incarnation, life, and death of Christ consummated the divine design of the covenant of redemption that emanated from the council of the Godhead before the foundation of the world.

Again, however, the Word of God stands against all such deviating suggestions. What, then, is to be said regarding the final questions we have raised? There is no entry to meaning, we conclude, on any level or in respect to any question that can engage our deliberation, other than what has been declared by the Word of God. Only therein do we have not only the sovereign declaration of God from whose hands we came and to whom we therefore stand in undeniable obligation, but we have in the Scriptures the only true and reliable criteria of knowledge and the principles of true interpretation. The key to the Scriptures is the understanding of the covenantal

---

[6] See A. A. Hodge, *Outlines of Theology*, 422. See also for an expansive treatment the same author's *The Atonement* (Grand Rapids: Baker, 1974). The issues that have been discussed in this connection in the preceding chapters are addressed in the classic work by James Buchanan, *The Doctrine of Justification* (Edinburgh: Banner of Truth, 1984).

dealings with us that God graciously designed from before the beginning, and which in due time he instituted for our benefit. Christ, his divine identity, his redemptive purpose and accomplishment, and his faithful discharge of his messianic assignment provide the key to the Scriptures. That is so, first, in the fact that the people of God were all along entrusted to the care of Christ, in their creation and in their conduct in this life, and in their eternal prospect and inheritance; second, in the promise of his coming that God gave to our first parents following their fall and in what that involved in God's dealing with his people in the Old Testament history of his administration of the covenant of grace; third, in the coming of Christ in the fullness of time and his active and passive obedience in this world; and fourth, in the administration of the kingdom of God that Christ effects in his heavenly High Priestly session.

In saying that, we hold, with orthodox doctrinal theology and with the implications that has for the Christian's life in this world, to the import of the old truths for which Athanasius, Augustine, and Anselm stood so definitively. That truth, at a minimum, is as follows. To Athanasius we owe the defense of the autotheotic nature of the Person Jesus Christ. He is the eternal Son of God, fully God, in whom resides the full essence of the Godhead. We are saved, if we are saved, by none other than the Second Person of the Godhead who became incarnate for our redemption.

To Augustine we owe the insistence on the fallenness of all those who descended from Adam by ordinary generation. We concur with his insistence, as a result, on the bondage of the will to Satan and sin. The will is not free in the sense that it is able to effect any individual action that has value to eternal good. It follows that we are saved, if we are saved, not by an autosoterism that emanates from the sovereign efficiency of our own will. Nor are we saved by a synergism that conjures an effective cooperation between the will and grace of God on the one hand and a certain strength of our own will on the other. We are saved by a divine monergism. That is the essence and the glory of the gospel.

To Anselm we owe the clarification that in his death Christ definitively saved his people by providing the only efficient satisfaction for their sin. We are saved, if we are saved, because in recognition of the death of Christ in real historical time the Holy Spirit of God applies the benefits of that death to those for whom Christ died. They were those whom God the Father gave to the Son to redeem before the foundation of the world.

A final question remains. It addresses the implications for practice and life of all that has been said to this point. The believer exists, the preceding chapter has concluded, in a new solidarity in Christ, in his membership of the church in which that solidarity comes to expression. What is to be said of the obligations that devolve on the believer as a result?

We are saved, if we are saved, by the effectual call of God's Spirit to us each individually. The responsibilities and obligations we sustain as members of the body of Christ are such as recognize the integrity of our individual personhood. But while that is so, and while we stand before God in the responsibility and accountability that our derivative personhood establishes, we do not live and comport ourselves in the church individualistically. In the solidarity in which we have been established, we who are members of the church are "members one of another" (Eph. 4:25).

The believer is to see, and to live in the context of the awareness of the fact, that he has been assumed by the grace of God into "the whole body [the church as the body of Christ] fitly joined together and compacted by that which every joint supplieth" (Eph. 4:16), into the organism of the church that God has redeemed. The purpose of that redemption and of that incorporation into the church is that God will be glorified in the salvation of his people. That, we have seen, will conduce to the glory of the Son. Of those who belong to Christ it is promised that they will "all come in the unity of the faith, and to the knowledge of the Son of God, unto a perfect man, unto the measure of the stature of the fulness of Christ" (Eph. 4:13). The glory of Christ is exhibited and the security of his saints is declared in Hebrews 9:15, "For this cause he [Christ] is the mediator of the new testament, that by means of death, for the redemption of the transgressions that were under the first testament, they which are called might receive the promise of eternal inheritance," or the inheritance that has been promised.

Perhaps there is no higher description of the identity of the Christian than that in the apostolic statement that God the Father has made us "accepted in the beloved [in Christ]" (Eph. 1:6). That confirms the new solidarity in which we have been incorporated in Christ. And in the light of that, the Christian believer now ponders the remarkable prophetic statement of Isaiah that Christ "shall see of the travail of his soul and shall be satisfied" (Is. 51:11). God the Father looks upon his Son and sees the saints whom he has redeemed; and Christ looks upon his saints and takes satisfaction in them and in his work of redemption of them. That is the height of the privilege to which those who have believed in Christ, in the repentance and faith that God the Holy Spirit communicates to them, enjoy. May God give us who belong to him grace to walk in the light of that high realization, and in accordance with the ethical imperatives that it conveys. Then we shall be "to the praise of the glory of his grace" (Eph. 1:6).[7]

---

[7] Readers familiar with trends in modern theology will realize that many of the doctrines I have discussed are currently subject to new interpretations in what has been referred to as the New Perspective on Paul (NPP). A significant but misleading rewriting of the apostolic doctrine has lately gained currency in the relevant literature. It projects erroneous claims regarding the doctrines of justification, the righteousness of God, the covenant of grace, and the reciprocal imputation that establishes redemption – the imputation of the sinner's sin to Christ and the imputation of Christ's righteousness to the sinner. A minimal entry to the extensive NPP literature is provided in E. P. Sanders, *Paul and*

Palestinian Judaism (Minneapolis: Fortress Press, 1977); N. T. Wright, *The Climax of the Covenant* (Minneapolis: Fortress Press, 1993), and *What Saint Paul Really Said* (Grand Rapids: Eerdmans, 1997); Guy Prentiss Waters, *Justification and the New Perspectives on Paul* (Phillipsburg: P&R, 2004); Richard B. Gaffin, Jr., "Paul the Theologian," *Westminster Theological Journal*, 2000, 121-141. Wright, for example, claims that "What Paul means by justification ... is not 'how you become a Christian,' so much as 'how you can tell who is a member of the covenant family'" (*What Saint Paul Really Said*, 122). "'Justification' in the first century was not about how someone might establish a relationship with God.... In standard Christian theological language, it wasn't so much about soteriology as about ecclesiology; not so much about salvation as about the church," ibid., 119. The shift of focus to ecclesiology is instanced in Wright's statement, "'the gospel' is not an account of how people get saved.... Let us be quite clear. 'The gospel' is the announcement of Jesus' lordship ... which works with power to bring people into the family of Abraham," ibid., 133. Wright's conclusion instances the NPP disclaimer of the reality and significance of forensic imputation: "If we use the language of the law court, it makes no sense whatever to say that the judge imputes, imparts, bequeaths, conveys or otherwise transfers his righteousness to either the plaintiff or the defendant. Righteousness is not an object, a substance or a gas which can be passed across the courtroom.... To imagine the defendant somehow receiving the judge's righteousness is simply a category mistake. That is not how the language works," ibid., 98. Wright holds, as he puts it, to "an ecclesiocentric hermeneutic in Paul where exegetes have traditionally seen a christocentric one," *The Climax of the Covenant*, 264. But a discussion of the full significance of the NPP focus on these issues, driven largely by a misplaced view of covenant membership, taking up Sanders' concept of "covenantal nomism," is beyond our present objectives. Considerable attention is given in the NPP literature to the manner in which Paul understood "the works of the law." Paul's problem, as a result and as the NPP sees it, was that of convincing the Jews that the Gentiles should be admitted to membership of the covenantal relation without subscription and obedience to the Jewish boundary, or identity, markers, circumcision and the food laws. But it is not possible to agree that Paul's conception of the works of the law was restricted in that sense. The NPP attempt to establish a new understanding of the relation of Paul to Second Temple Judaism (515BC-70AD), an attempt that would, if successful, require the conclusion that the traditional Reformed theological reading of Paul has been seriously in error, is itself without merit.

Index of Scripture References

Genesis
1:26-28	30
1:28	37, 66
2:17	31, 61
2:19-20	37
3:8	35, 40, 41, 82
3:15	34, 44, 129
3:24	83
6:5	12
9:6	180
15:5	138
15:6	70
15:9	32
17:1	36
22:17	138
50:20	104

Exodus
19:6	159

Leviticus
11:44	166
18:5	45

Numbers
12:7-8	41
15:30-31	159

Deuteronomy
17:2-7	159
18:15	41

Job
9:1	3

Psalms
2:7	133
14:1	19
24:1	171
33:11	104
36:9	127
50:10	172
51:5	10
89:4	133
110:3	88

Proverbs
21:1-2	104
22:2	172
26:11	87

Isaiah
5:8	172
45:7	104
51:11	185
55:8	116

Jeremiah
17:9	13, 38

Ezekiel
9:3-4	116
20:11	69

Hosea
6:7	45

Joel
2:25	104

Amos
8:4-6   172

Haggai
2:8   171

Matthew
1:21   27
3:17   142
4:17   97
16:13   177
16:16   178
16:18   177
16:19   167
20:28   182

Mark
10:45   182

Luke
9:35   142
11:21   38, 86

John
1:18   105, 129
3:8   97
3:13   130, 135
3:36   38
6:67-69   178
8:34   13, 87
8:36   105
8:44   10, 38, 87
10:3   136
10:11   136
10:20   136
10:26   136
10:30   142
14:10   115
14:18   131
15:26   144
17:1   132
17:5   8, 132
17:6   46, 115, 136, 150
17:9   136
17:12   164
17:20   131, 136

Acts
2:23   118
4:28   118
7:38   156
14:23   169
16:31   97
17:30   97
20:28   8, 145, 146, 150, 169

Romans
1:17   4
1:18   20, 163
1:21-25   20
1:30   13, 40, 64, 84
2:13   45
3:25   137
3:26   137
5:1   64, 67, 137
5:12   37, 146, 181
5:12-21   149
5:14   56
5:19   34, 105
6:16   38, 87
6:17   94
8:1   67, 137
8:7   64
8:20-22   145
9:5   9, 129
9:6   159
11:35   70
12:5   166

1 Corinthians
1:30   95
2:7   116

Index of Scripture References

2:9	124	2:9	9, 130
2:14	13, 38, 85, 126	4:5	174
10:31	40, 174		
11:29	83	**1 Thessalonians**	
12:25-27	166	4:12	174
15:22	150		
		1 Timothy	
2 Corinthians		3:1	170
4:4	12, 38, 85	3:15	170
4:6	86	3:16	129
Galatians		**2 Timothy**	
3:24	158	2:12	141
3:29	138	4:2	168, 170
4:4	35		
		Titus	
Ephesians		1:5	169
1:4	8, 118, 136, 166	1:6	170
1:5-6	117		
1:6	166, 185	**Hebrews**	
1:9	144	1:2	132
1:10	141, 144, 145	1:3	66, 131
1:11	104	2:17	137
1:12	117	5:5	133
2:1	38	6:4-5	164
2:8	4, 15, 57, 94	6:4-6	154, 163
2:18	65	6:17	32
4:13	185	9:14	115
4:16	184	9:15	99, 137, 185
4:25	184	10:26-29	164
5:25	145, 150	10:29	160
		12:14	100
Philippians		13:21	147
2:9	71		
2:12-13	100	**James**	
4:7	93	3:9	180
Colossians		**1 Peter**	
1:15-16	141	1:2	118
1:17	64	1:15-16	166
2:3	64, 91	2:9	159, 166

3:15	174	3:2	65
		3:4	38
2 Peter		3:9	85
2:22	87	4:1-2	129
3:8	133	4:10	8, 137
3:18	166		
		Revelation	
1 John		5:10	66, 141
2:2	137	13:8	161
2:19	154, 164	17:8	161

Index of Names

Alexander, A., 110
Alexander of Alexandria, 7
Andradius, 110
Anselm, 4, 17, 18-22, 106, 182, 183, 184
Aquinas, T., 12, 108, 109, 111
Aristotle, 108
Arius, 7, 22, 178, 179
Armstrong, J.H., 90
Athanasius, 4, 7, 8, 22, 24, 129, 134, 177, 183
Augustine, 4, 10, 11, 14, 15, 22, 23, 67, 75, 79, 86, 133, 139, 180, 183

Bahnsen, G.L., 108, 113, 116
Bannerman, J., 157-159, 162
Battles, F.L., 4
Bavinck, H., 16, 30
Beale, G.K., 45
Beeke, J.R., 11, 29, 79
Berkhof, L., 29, 36, 121
Bibza, J., 45
Boston, T., 16, 33, 59
Brunner, E., 181
Buchanan, J., 182

Calvin, J., 4, 50, 68-72, 79, 86, 92, 93, 94, 116, 121
Chadwick, H., 133
Chauncy, C., 92
Chemnitz, M., 111
Cherry, C., 12, 92
Cole, H., 79

Cowper, W., 177
Cunningham, W., 6, 7, 11, 15, 86, 88-90, 130, 134, 135, 142
Currid, J.D., 45

Dabney, R.L., 58, 67, 139
Dallimore, A., 11, 79
Davie, D., 177
Descartes, R., 18
Dodd, C.H., 180
Dowey, E.A., 116

Edwards, J., 11, 76, 77, 81, 88, 92-94, 131
Einstein, A., 75, 76, 101

Ferguson, S., 11, 29, 59, 67, 79
Fisher, E., 16, 28, 33, 35, 45
Flavel, J., 5
Flew, A., 76, 101
Frame, J., 91, 108, 109
Fuller, D., 50, 52, 53, 54, 55, 59, 60-63

Gaffin, R.B., 53, 186
Gaunilo, 18
Gerstner, J., 19, 108
Godfrey, W.R., 55
Gundry, R., 51
Gurnall, W., 5

Hafemann, S.J., 50, 53, 54
Hägglund, B., 130

Harnack, A., 13, 14
Helm, P., 139
Hendriksen, W., 130
Henry, C.F.H., 79
Henry, M., 5
Hodge, A.A., 29, 46, 48, 49, 67, 182
Hodge, C., 29, 49, 67
Hoffeker, W.A., 45
Hughes, S., 2

Jeon, J.K., 68
Johnston, O.R., 13, 85

Kant, I., 19, 31, 108
Karlberg, M., 28, 59, 72, 73
Kendall, R.T., 139
King, J., 70
Kline, M., 28, 32, 47, 50, 55, 57, 61, 62, 68

Lillback, P.A., 48, 68-71
Lindsley, A., 19, 108
Lloyd-Jones, D.M., 94
Lund, G.J., 130
Luther, M., 4, 13, 85, 121

Macleod, J., 16
Manton, T., 5
Maritain, J., 110
McNeill, J.T., 4
Millar, J., 14
Mitchell, E.K., 13
Murray, J., 28, 31, 59, 67, 68, 71, 84, 116, 149, 167, 172, 180, 181
Myers, T., 70

Newman, J.H., 34
Noll, M.A., 152

Owen, J., 12, 31, 59, 67, 71, 139

Packer, J.I., 13, 85
Pelagius, 10, 11, 14, 15, 75, 79, 181
Peterson, R.A., 178
Pighius, A., 79
Piper, J., 50-52, 54, 91, 131
Poole, M., 5, 93
Praxeas, 115
Pringle, J., 72

Reymond, R.L., 18, 36, 45, 46, 61, 139
Robertson, O.P., 16, 55, 62

Sabellius, 6
Sanders, E.P., 185, 186
Schaff, P., 4, 15, 17, 18, 20, 21
Shedd, W.G.T., 6, 8, 17, 21, 58, 67, 116
Shepherd, N., 16, 63
Spinoza, B., 76
Sproul, R.C., 14, 19, 108, 165
Strimple, R.B., 90

Thornwell, J.H., 56-58
Tillich, P., 109, 110
Trumper, T.J.R., 68
Turretin, F., 5, 7, 15, 30, 36, 59, 67, 71, 81, 83, 88, 91, 96, 122, 157

Vande Kapelle, R.P., 45
Van Til, C., 10, 37, 102, 108-113, 116, 119-123, 139-141
Vickers, D., 12, 31, 80, 84,

91, 139, 142, 146, 172
Vos, G., 35, 53, 60, 146

Ward, R.S., 49
Wardlaw, R., 162
Waters, G.P., 186
Watson, R., 140
Wells, D.F., 152, 175, 176
Wells, H.G., 3

Wesley, J., 11, 79
Westcott, S.P., 31
Whitefield, G., 11, 79
Witsius, H., 5, 17, 33, 49, 54, 71
Wright, N.T., 186
Wright, R.K.M., 90

Young, E.J., 41, 104

Index of Subjects

Ability
  moral, 77, 78, 81, 88
  natural, 77, 78, 81, 88
Abortion, 171, 173
Absolute being, 113
Absolute meaning, 113
Absolute personhood, 113
Abstraction, 120
Adamic offices, 36, 37, 42, 43, 44
  federal headship, 3, 37, 84
Agnosticism, 133
Amyraldianism, 155, 181
Analogia entis, 107-109, 111
Analogical knowledge, 124
Anthropology, biblical, 11
Antinomianism, 63
Apologetics
  Reformed, 146
  transcendental, 101, 103
Apostolic examples, 169
Apostolic literature, 169
Arianism, 6, 7, 11, 130
Arminianism, 79, 90, 92, 95, 155, 180
Atheism, 78, 81
Atonement, 4, 20, 73, 97, 106
  governmental theory of, 182
  moral theory of, 182
  necessity of, 5, 17, 20
  particular, 136, 139
  satisfaction for sin, 21, 44
  satisfaction theory of, 5, 18, 182
  substitutionary, 21
  universal, 137
Autonomy, 12, 31, 40, 44, 74, 78, 79, 83, 102, 103, 125, 126, 138
  epistemological, 40, 78, 102
  ethical, 40, 78, 102
  metaphysical, 40, 78, 102
Autosoterism, 14, 15, 96, 102, 183

Baptism, 157
Being in general, 111
Benediction, 27, 31, 32, 34, 54, 82
Bias, 91
Bondage, 97
  of the will, 98, 99

Canons of Dordt, 79
Categories
  of explanation, 39, 65, 147
  of understanding, 40
Chain of being, 107, 110
Children, 157, 159
Christ
  agent of creation, 141
  ascension of, 128
  atonement of, 4
  autotheotic nature of, 5, 7, 9, 22, 142, 183
  communication of
    properties of natures, 178
  cosmic significance of, 24, 129, 132, 139, 141, 143, 144, 147

covenantal commitment of, 135
divine person, 178
eternal generation of, 134
glorification of, 132, 142
glory of, 65, 135
good shepherd, 136
heavenly session of, 128
high priestly office of, 9, 24, 47, 183
high priestly prayer, 136, 164
human nature of, 65, 128, 135
impeccability of, 136
incarnation of, 128, 135
intercession of, 65
kingship of, 172
Lord of the covenant, 47
messianic-redemptive assignment of, 3, 129, 132, 140, 183
mystery of, 132
obedience of
  active, 9, 62, 135, 141
  passive, 9, 135
offices of
  king, 36, 47, 66, 146
  prophet, 36, 40, 47, 146
  priest, 36, 40, 41, 47, 65, 146
omnipresence of, 131
penal sacrifice of, 140
personhood of, 3, 6, 10, 21, 24, 132, 178
preeminence of, 147
preexistence of, 129
redeemer-king, 177
resurrection of, 128
satisfaction of, 44, 106
self-existence of, 134
sinlessness of, 135
substitute, 27, 36, 37, 40, 46, 47, 66
substitute punishment of, 137
substitutionary death of, 9
substitutionary obedience of, 58, 62
union with, 24, 145, 150
Christological
  controversies, 11
  settlement, 9
Christology, 21, 143
Church, 144-146, 150, 175
  a constitutional monarchy, 169
  credible profession in, 161
  elders of, 161, 165, 169
  nurture of the saints, 169
  external covenant in, 157, 158, 160, 162
  internal covenant in, 157, 159, 160, 162
  invisible aspect of, 24, 151, 154, 156, 162
  mandate of, 170
  membership of, 150, 153, 154, 156, 166
  not a democracy, 169
  office of, 167
  organic entity of, 151
  visible aspect of, 24, 151, 154, 156, 159, 160, 162
Circumcision, 32
Common grace, 66, 91, 143
Compatibilism, 104
Congregationalism, 151
Continuity, 107, 114
  epistemological, 111, 112
  metaphysical, 107, 108, 110, 111

Index of Subjects

of being, 107, 109
of knowledge, 107
Corruption of nature, 39
Council of Chalcedon, 9, 134, 179
Council of Ephesus, 15
Council of Nicea, 7, 8
Council of Trent, 181
Covenant, 23, 27
  of creation, 10, 23, 66
  of grace, 28, 46, 47, 49, 53, 54, 60, 70, 72, 153, 156, 162, 183
  of redemption, 49, 115, 154, 156, 163
  of works, 10, 23, 27-29, 33, 35, 42-73, 82, 141
  dissent from, 56, 58
  Godward aspect of, 43, 44
  Sinaitic, 27
Covenantal obedience, 30
Covenantal nomism, 186
Covenantal obligations, 23, 26, 31, 36, 39, 74, 180
Covenantal overlay, 47
Covenantal relations, 32
Covenant theology, 47, 48, 50, 55, 63, 154
Creation, 3, 80, 101, 110, 128, 143, 144, 183
Creator-creature distinction, 56, 107, 109, 112-114, 119, 124
Creator-creature relation, 29, 56
  analogical, 119
  equivocal, 119
  univocal, 119
Creaturehood, 30, 78
Culture, 143, 144, 168, 173, 175, 176

Curse, 32, 64

Decalogue, 35, 173
Depravity, 12, 77, 88, 98
Derivative being, 113
Derivative knowledge, 113
Derivative personhood, 113
Determinism, 127
Deus absconditus, 121
Deus revelatus, 121
Dialecticism
  rationalist-irrationalist, 112
Discontinuity, 114
  epistemological, 113, 114, 119, 124
  metaphysical, 113, 114
Discrimination, 171
Divine decrees, 115
Divine-human relation, 54, 55, 107, 112
Divinization, 108, 109
Dominion, 30, 37, 42, 66
Donum superadditum, 110

Economics, 2, 171, 172
  concentration of power, 172
  deprivation, 175
  exploitation, 172
Ecumenicity, 153
Effectual calling, 102, 155, 156, 184
Election, 125, 155, 161
Enlightenment, 2
Enmity, 64
Epistemic capacity, 111, 133
Epistemology, 78, 112
Equity, 171
Erastianism, 151
Eschatological hope, 66, 144, 151
Eschatological terminus, 145

Eternal security, 141
Eternity, 132
Ethical criteria, 75
Ethical imperatives, 179
Ethical lapse, 38, 110
Ethical mandates, 38
Evangelical awakening, 79
Evangelicalism, 12, 14, 79, 152, 170

Facts, 65
  Christological interpretation of, 147
Faculties of the soul, 10, 26, 74, 82, 88, 97, 98, 125
  affective, 93
  depravity of, 12, 77, 88, 98
  emotional, 13, 26, 74, 77, 83, 91, 93, 98
  harmony of, 83, 99
  intellectual, 12, 26, 74, 77, 82, 83, 91, 98
  originative, 91
  volitional, 13, 26, 74, 83, 98, 102
Faculty psychology, 92
Faith, 99, 161, 185
  refuge of, 4, 127, 137
Fall, 3, 12, 22, 27, 74, 101, 111, 125, 176
False professors, 154, 157, 159, 160, 162-164
Fatalism, 127
Federal headship, 37, 180
Federalism, 28
Federal theology, 48, 68, 70, 71
Filioque clause, 7
Finitude, 65, 140
Forensic guilt, 51
Forensic justification, 63, 95

Forensic righteousness, 51
Free agency, 81, 86, 87
Free will, 13, 14, 22, 23, 75, 78, 80, 81, 86, 98, 99, 101
Fuller-Piper thesis, 54

Gnosticism, 130
God
  actions of, 121
  attributes of, 120, 121
    communicable, 84
    incommunicable, 84
  binding of, 57, 70, 71, 72
  communication with, 41
  communion with, 65, 81
  compassion of, 20
  condescension of, 57
  creator, 2, 3
  decreeing, 24, 120, 122
  decrees of, 80, 107, 115, 120, 122, 123, 155, 156
    subjects of, 155, 157
  essence of, 6, 8, 121
  existence of, 17
  glory of, 41
  grace of, 56-58, 61, 69, 72
  holiness of, 38
  honor of, 20
  immanence of, 3, 131
  justice of, 56-58, 61, 69, 72
  knowability of, 121
  knowledge of, 121
  love of, 20
  mercy of, 20
  ordinations of, 115, 120, 121
  personal, 76, 101
  purposes of, 120, 121
  revelation of, 103, 116, 119
  simplicity of, 155
  sovereignty of, 75, 123

Index of Subjects

timelessness of, 121, 140
transcendence of, 3, 179
unity of, 155
will of, 123
  decretive, 105, 126
  preceptive, 105
  work of creation, 131
  work of providence, 131
  wrath of, 140
Godhead
  consubstantiality of, 6, 7
  council of, 24, 100, 118, 154, 155
  distinguishable properties of, 142
  essence of, 139
  oneness of, 134
  ontological, 142
  redemptive offices of, 115, 135
  threeness of, 134
  trinity of, 134
  unity of, 134
Grace, 53, 98
  of creation, 57
  primacy of, 68
Greatest apparent good, 92
Guilt, 52, 180

Habitus, 83, 98
Hegemony
  of the church, 151
  of the emotions, 84, 92
  of the mind, 84, 92
Hermeneutical principle, 48
Holiness, 26, 30, 54, 81, 99
  original, 39, 42
Holy Spirit, 97, 98, 100, 102, 115, 127, 130, 138, 143, 150, 155, 156, 163, 184, 185
  autotheotic, 142
  preparatory work of, 163
Humanism, 1, 2, 153
Human responsibility, 75

Image of God, 30, 80, 97, 109, 180
Immutability, 84, 100
Impeccability, 84
Imputation, 51
  of guilt, 3, 10, 51, 84, 95, 146
  of righteousness, 51, 95
  of sin, 3, 10
  reciprocal, 63, 136, 137, 180
Independency, 162
Intratrinitarian
  communication, 132, 139, 141

Justification, 4, 62, 63, 73, 101
  forensic, 16, 63, 95

Keys of the kingdom, 167
Knowledge, 113, 114

Laws
  of being, 147
  of operation, 147
Legalism, 63
Levitical priesthood, 41
Libertarianism, 105
Logic, 133
  laws of, 91
  timebound, 133

Malediction, 27, 31, 54, 82
Man
  analogue of God, 113, 126
  creation of, 29
  depravity of, 77, 88, 98

derivative
  being, 113
  knowledge, 113
  personhood, 113
divinization of, 108, 109
dominion of, 30, 37, 42
God-hater, 87
image of God, 30, 80, 97, 109, 180
metaphysical status, 38
nature of, 10
offices of
  king, 36, 42-44, 64
  prophet, 36, 39, 42-44, 64
  priest, 36, 42-44, 64
perfectibility of, 2
postlapsarian, 53, 54
prelapsarian, 53, 54
probation of, 31, 32, 34
vicegerent, 30
Materialism, 1
Merit, 44, 52, 67-71
  imputation of, 72
Meritorious obedience, 56, 69, 71
Meritorious works, 57
Monergism, 15
  divine, 15, 96, 184
  human, 15
Morality, 176
Moral law, 173
Mosaic administration, 41, 72
Mosaic covenant, 73
Murder, 173
Mystery, 23, 24, 101, 103, 104, 124, 130, 144, 178
  of Godliness, 129

Neoevangelicalism, 79
Neonomianism, 16
Neoplatonism, 109

New Perspective on Paul, 185, 186
Nicene Creed, 7

Obedience, 28, 32, 43, 56, 61
  meritorious, 56, 69, 71
Ontological proof, 17, 18
Ontological trinity, 143
Openness of God, 170
Open theism, 90, 105, 170
Opera ad extra, 115, 135
Opera ad intra, 135

Paganism, 2
Patripassianism, 116
Pelagian-Augustine controversy, 14
Pelagianism, 11, 12, 14, 16, 95, 99, 111
  semi-pelagianism, 11, 12, 16, 96, 99
Perdition, 97, 164
Personhood
  derivative, 30, 113
Posse non peccare, 81, 82, 84
Possibility, 122
Postmodernism, 153
Poverty, 2
Predestination, 75, 76, 97, 117
Predication
  principles of, 40, 65, 147
Prelapsarian state, 49, 53
Presbyterianism, 151
Probability, 122
Probation, 44, 66
Prophetic office, 39, 146
Propitiation, 8, 41
Providence, 75, 80, 131, 143

Reason in general, 111

Index of Subjects

Redemption, 3, 24, 101
  accomplishment of, 27
  possibility of, 118, 120, 122, 123
Reformation, 4, 47
Reformed theology, 5, 15, 27, 48, 61, 103, 106, 107, 121, 122
Regeneration, 15, 61, 80, 86, 95, 98, 100, 150, 165
Remonstrant theology, 11, 79, 95
Repentance, 161, 164, 165, 185
Revelation
  anthropomorphic, 103, 116, 119
Righteousness, 26

Sabbath, 35, 173
Sabellianism, 6, 11, 130
Sacrament, 82
Sacrifice, 41, 140
Salvation
  efficient cause, 4, 95
  essence of, 63
  evidence of, 63
  instrumental cause, 4, 95
  meritorious cause, 4, 95
Sanctification, 16, 62, 63, 99, 100, 101, 169
Scientific methodology, 2
Second Adam, 56, 58, 66, 72
Second Temple Judaism, 186
Self-consciousness, 37, 78, 109
Semen religionis, 19
Sensus deitatis, 19, 163
Sin, 3, 31, 125
  depravation of, 145
  deprivation of, 145
  doctrine of, 125, 181
  entailment of, 64, 94, 148, 167
  ethical lapse, 38, 110
  penalty for, 138
  state of, 39
Socinianism, 89, 90, 182
Solidarity, 149, 150, 166, 184
  in Adam, 24, 149, 150
  in Christ, 24, 150, 184, 185
  in the church, 166, 184
Soteriology, 17, 21, 27, 34
Speculation, 103
Subordinationism, 142
  economic, 142
  ontological, 142
Summum bonum, 35
Synergism, 14, 96, 102, 183
Synod of Alexandria, 7
Synod of Dordt, 11, 181

Taxation, 171
Ten Commandments, 36, 172
Time, 65, 123, 133, 135, 139, 143, 144, 156, 179
Timelessness, 121, 132, 140
Transmission of nature, 84, 146
Tree of life, 82
  sacramental significance of, 82, 83

Union with Christ, 24, 145, 150, 151
Unitarianism, 130

Vicegerent, 20

Watershed of history, 128
Will
  autonomy of, 80

bondage of, 98, 99
freedom of, 76, 78, 99
of God, 105, 126

Works principle, 28, 33, 44, 45, 52, 55, 61, 62, 72, 73
Worship, 35

www.ingramcontent.com/pod-product-compliance
Lightning Source LLC
Chambersburg PA
CBHW021100080526
44587CB00010B/321